To Hal

INTRODUCTION

This edition is in celebration of the centennial of the purchase of *The New York Times* by Adolph S. Ochs.

When I was a youngster I was raised on the story of how my grandfather, Adolph Ochs, came to be a newspaperman. It was a fear of ghosts.

Young Adolph, it seems, had a menial job in a local print shop. His route home passed by the local cemetery, and his hours were such that he would have had to walk by that spooky spot just at the hour when the ghosts were also said to walk.

So the only logical thing for Adolph to do was to hang around the print shop after work so he could walk home with the shop foreman, who lived in the same neighborhood.

Each evening Adolph waited about two hours for his walking companion. During that period, to while away the time, he learned to set type. This skill led to other jobs in the print industry and finally from the Chattanooga *Times* to *The New York Times*.

As we celebrate Mr. Ochs's transformation of the *Times* 100 years ago, we should not forget to tip our hats to those spooky ghosts who made it all possible.

> Arthur Ochs Sulzberger
> Chairman
> The New York Times Company

AN OPENING NOTE

This book was written early in the 1960s, not long after I retired as a reporter for *The New York Times* to raise a family. When I went to work there, just seven years had elapsed since the death of Adolph Ochs, and his presence still seemed to pervade the atmosphere—in the city room, we tapped out our stories on battered old non-electric typewriters, and nobody dreamed that computers would in a few decades revolutionize at least the mechanics of putting out his great newspaper.

Even so, I have done only a limited amount of updating because it struck me, upon rereading what I'd written from the perspective of 1996, that a good part of its appeal came from its reflection of attitudes and values still very similar to those of Ochs's era.

Lest I seem to have ignored any of his precepts about accuracy, though, I must specify that the pages that follow contain fact not fiction, although to add flavor I sprinkled conversations here and there, particularly in the first, mood-setting chapter. Nevertheless, there and wherever else a person speaks in quotes, the words are taken either from letters Ochs wrote or the memory of his close relatives.

Among these relatives, who provided most of the personal anecdotes about Ochs, were three no longer with us: his cherished daughter, Iphigene Ochs Sulzberger; her husband, Arthur Hays Sulzberger, publisher of *The New York Times* during my years there; and his son-in-law, Orvil E. Dryfoos, who succeeded him as publisher, and who helped a great deal by making various files and privately printed memoirs available to me.

In addition, I must thank Ochs's granddaughters Marian Heiskell and Ruth Holmberg for sharing some of their memories, and the latter, who was publisher of the Chattanooga *Times,* steered me, too, to valuable source material about the Chattanooga phase of her grandfather's career. Also, an old friend of mine from the *Times* city room, John N. Popham, who became executive managing editor of the Chattanooga *Times*, was very helpful, and the director of the *Times*'s libraries during the period I was doing my research, Chester Lewis, provided much kind assistance, as did several members of his staff.

Finally, on every phase of the original manuscript's preparation, as well as its reappearance in this new edition, I have had the invaluable advice of the longtime *New York Times* editor and writer who is my husband. To him, this book is once more dedicated.

Doris Faber, February 1996

1

The attic bedroom had one tiny window. Not a trace of light showed through it yet, but the boy was wide awake. Propping himself on an elbow, he stared up at the small, gray square where the first glow of dawn would have to appear soon, for this night certainly could not last much longer. In cots at his left, his two younger brothers went on drawing the slow, even breaths of deep sleep. They were still babies, they could sleep. Not he.

Then suddenly a muffled step sounded on the steep wood stairs in the hall. The boy sat up swiftly. He watched the door of the little attic room being opened with care, to keep its protesting squeak as soft as possible.

Captain Julius Ochs peered into the dimness.

"All right, son," he said. "It's four o'clock. Time to be starting."

"Yes, Papa," the boy murmured as his father retreated.

With a burst of the energy he had been straining to hold in, the lad leaped from bed and grabbed his shabby shirt. Shabby would be too kind a word for the pair of pants he hurriedly stepped into—they were no color at all after endless washings, and they obviously had started their career man-sized, then been snipped and sewed to fit a boy.

It was no disgrace, though, to be wearing such hand-me-downs in Tennessee in 1869. It was four years after the ruinous Civil War, which had taken a fearful toll of the state's men and wealth, and new clothes were a rare sight. Without any qualms about how he would look, the boy hasti-ly finished dressing.

He was through as soon as he donned shirt and trousers, for at the moment he didn't have any shoes—his last win-ter's pair had already been passed on to a cousin they would fit. It was September now, and still warm, and going barefoot was no particular hardship, but if he were to keep on at school he would need a pair soon. That was part of the rea-son why he was getting up so early on this autumn morning.

Downstairs, his sturdy, dark-haired mother already stood bustling at the stove.

"No, Ma," he said. "Didn't we say I'd come *back* for breakfast after? This way everybody will be up."

"At least for the first time you'll have something in your stomach before you go," Mrs. Bertha Ochs said firmly.

She thrust a dish before him with chunks of her wonder-ful bread, soaked in a special egg for the occasion and fried. She looked questioningly at her husband, who sat silently sipping from a mug of steaming coffee—and he nodded. She quickly filled another mug with coffee, then set it down before their son.

The boy's face, pale and serious beneath his jet black mop of most unboyish curls, burst into a grin. No warm milk for him today, or milk flavored with a few spoonfuls of coffee. This morning he was getting all coffee, without even asking.

"Thanks, Ma," he said.

"There's a chill out so early," she explained, shrugging.

Captain Ochs pushed aside his own coffee mug and shook his head slowly as if to chase an unpleasant thought. His handsome, bearded face wore a sad, almost bewildered frown, as well it might. In recent years he had watched one business venture after another fail, making a mockery of his dreams of seeing his sons well-educated, respected men of substance in the community.

True, his dry goods store had flashed to a brief prosperity right after the war, and he had set his family up in a fine house with two servants and two horses. It was a small country estate, which he proudly called Ochsenburg, where there were books, music, thoughtful conversation among distinguished guests.

Then overnight prices had plummeted from war-scarcity peaks. The great bolts of cloth he had stocked at inflated dollars would bring only a fraction of what he had paid for them, and he took a terrible loss. Now there was no more store, no more fine house, only this unpainted shack on Water Street on the outskirts of Knoxville.

The kindest, the most upright of men, a natural scholar who could speak six languages, the captain was out of his depth in the rough and tumble of post-war Tennessee. Now, as a justice of the peace taking in fees of only a dollar or two a day, he was earning scarcely enough to feed his six children. Small wonder that his face wore a sad look this morning as his oldest son prepared to assume a man's estate too soon.

"Come," Captain Ochs said to the boy. "It's time we go."

The boy glanced at his father inquiringly. The whole idea of the job had been his own—and both parents had objected at first, although, like wearing old clothes, going to work young was no disgrace in Tennessee. He almost grinned as he thought back to the way they had fretted before giving in, complaining he would be too tired for school. Now they were making such a fuss over him!

"This morning, I'll come with you," his father said in a strange tone mingling pride and disappointment.

Father and son rose then, and the boy noticed with a surge of manly superiority that his younger brothers had crept down the stairs to watch the departure. Two of his sisters huddled back of them. Only the baby still slept, not knowing of the great thing happening this morning.

With a wave and a brave smile, the boy walked beside his father in the cool, misty dawn. Dew lay damply on the dust of the walk, and the street looked strangely lonesome with not a soul about yet, only a few early-rising chickens scratching in the next yard. The boy felt a small shiver as he hurried along beside his father.

After a block they turned away from the river—the mighty Tennessee that had borne flotillas of Federal gunboats not too long ago—and headed toward the center of town.

Closed, empty-seeming houses loomed in the mist; even the dogs that usually yipped around were quiet. It was unearthly still passing the Presbyterian cemetery, and even with his father at his side the boy had trouble forcing down the scary idea that maybe a ghost would pop out any minute. Then they came to a house with the smoke from a breakfast fire already curling up from the chimney. Forgetting all about the ghosts, the boy smiled to himself. He knew who lived there.

Just as they were passing the front door, it opened and a tall, chunky, yellow-haired youth emerged, whistling.

Captain Ochs said: "Is that the Widow Blake's boy who told you about this?"

His son nodded as Freckles Blake leaped over the low, sagging picket fence in front of his house, calling: "Hey, Muley, wait up!"

"Muley" was a slang word then for cows or oxen without horns, and the Ochs's name, spoken, sounded like "ox," so the boy was used to this nickname. He turned to see if his father would be disturbed, but he didn't seem to have heard.

"Muley, you coming to work?" Freckles asked.

The boy inclined his head slightly, and the solemn Captain Ochs and the two boys walked on silently. Soon they were stepping onto the chill, dusty cobblestones of Market Square.

Suddenly other boys were about, and the mist seemed to be lifting. Whistling, joshing, pushing, the boys were making for an alley along one side of a faded, one-story brick building—the small, untidy home of the Knoxville *Chronicle*.

The newspaper's side door off the alley was open. A clatter and rattle sounded within, and a rich, sharp smell filled the air. Sniffing that unforgettable aroma of printer's ink for the first time, Muley Ochs pressed on with the Widow Blake's son. He hardly noticed his own father had stopped beside the building across the alley.

A voice inside called one name, then another, and each boy stepped forward to perform the first part of his job. As fresh, unfolded papers came sliding from the clattering press, he folded, counted fifty. Then with his stack under his arm, he trudged four or five miles to deliver those fifty papers to fifty homes before going back to his own home for breakfast—and then on to school, if he came from a family that held with scrimping to pay for schooling; there were few free schools in Tennessee then.

At last the voice called: "Ochs!"

The crowd had shrunk by then. Only bearded Captain Ochs was left standing across the alley, watching as his son stepped in and began gingerly lifting and folding the newspapers.

In a few seconds the boy's fingers were smudgy with still-damp ink. Once when he raised his hand to push his curly black hair back from his forehead, he left a dark smudge over one eye. All unaware and concentrating on his count, he hurried till his stack totaled fifty.

Then the aproned man guarding the press muttered: "You know you get twenty-five cents a day, a dollar and a half at the end of the week." There was no Sunday *Chronicle*; it came out just six days.

The boy nodded eagerly.

With his heart pounding, Adolph Simon Ochs picked up his stack of newspapers—and started out on one of the most remarkable careers in American newspaper history. He was, then, eleven years old.

2

Adolph Simon Ochs was born on March 12, 1858, in Cincinnati, Ohio. He was the second son of Julius and Bertha Levy Ochs, but shortly after his birth his toddler brother died; then the mantle of the eldest son, the main hope of his hopeful parents, was his.

His father and mother were new Americans, from respectable German-Jewish backgrounds. At the age of nineteen, Julius Ochs had left his native land because, being Jewish, he was not allowed to start his own bookbinding business after learning the trade as an apprentice; members of his faith had fewer privileges than other Germans then, although they were not treated with the savagery that erupted many years later in the Hitler era. Dark-eyed Bertha Levy had a more compelling reason for crossing the ocean. At the age of sixteen she had joined a secret group working to overthrow the despotic government, and during a street riot she had boldly dipped her handkerchief in the blood of a wounded fighter to flaunt her sympathy for his cause. That brought police to her house. To avoid prison, her family hastily packed and left for America.

Gentle and scholarly Julius Ochs became a traveling salesman in the New World, then a French and German teacher at the Mount Sterling, Kentucky, Female Institute. After only a year of teaching, he quit at the outbreak of the Mexican War, and volunteered for Army duty to show his gratitude to his new land. Bookish though he was, he made a good drillmaster because he had been trained for military service overseas. When he was mustered out, he wandered to Nashville in Tennessee selling dry goods. There he met Bertha Levy.

By then, pretty, serious Bertha was an ardent Southerner. Roaming through the South, the young salesman had come to hate slavery and was a stanch northern supporter in the quarrel that was to bring on the Civil War. But despite their political differences, the two fell in love and were married.

Fittingly enough, they set up housekeeping in Cincinnati, in the solid Union state of Ohio, but just across the river from slave-owning Kentucky. There they lived happily, if simply, for several years. When he became a father, Julius Ochs was the chief traveler for a wholesale jewelry firm, with a sales route that took him all over Ohio, Indiana and Kentucky. The making of money eluded him; he could not seem to guess right in business, and he tried one unsuccessful venture after another—till the Civil War put a stop to his dreamy drifting.

At the firing on Fort Sumter, Julius Ochs donned uniform again, joining the 52nd Ohio Volunteers. Because of his experience, he was assigned to training green troops.

Loyal as he was to the Stars and Stripes, Captain Ochs never was able to change his wife's loyalty to the Stars and Bars. Once during the war, when malaria raged among southern soldiers, Bertha Levy Ochs managed to get a package of quinine and hid it in the family baby buggy. Then she marched the buggy to a bridge over the Ohio River, intending to deliver the medicine to Confederate forces on the other side while pretending merely to air one of her infants.

Union sentries stopped her and kept her from crossing the bridge, though they did not arrest her. In later years, her children loved hearing this story, and Adolph would cheerfully insist, "I was in the buggy, wasn't I, Ma?" Then his younger brother, George, would say, with better reason, "No, I was!"

After the war, Captain Ochs and his wife agreed on a big move. They felt it their duty to help rebuild the battered South, and they had been taken by the surpassing beauty of the Smoky Mountain country of eastern Tennessee. So it was to this former battleground that they set their sights. They bought a covered wagon and jounced down to Knoxville.

But Captain Ochs was the wrong man to make a mark in that lately besieged river trading town where the scars of war still struck every eye. Even the grandeur of the mountains seemed dimmed, for on nearby slopes not a tree remained; they had been cut to clear a path for cannon, or to provide fuel for freezing Federals or Confederates. In the town, people scrounged for food and rags. A dreamer and a scholar, Captain Ochs lacked the dash and drive that other, tougher men would summon to put Knoxville back on the commerce map of the southeast.

But within the crowded rooms of the shack on Water Street where the Ochs family lived after his first dry goods store failed, the captain was never thought of as a failure. A wise man, a good man, the leader of the tiny Jewish community in town and esteemed by his other neighbors, he had the respect of his wife and children despite his lack of money-making talent.

"True worth is not measured by money," Bertha Levy Ochs taught her children.

Still, a certain amount of money was essential, even in a day when eggs cost only ten cents a dozen. Julius Ochs never learned how to pay for all the eggs his family could eat and still not compromise his ideals. But his son Adolph would show him a way.

A wiry, energetic boy, young Adolph combined the best of both of his parents—his father's mind and heart, his mother's bustling competence. Compared with other boys, Muley seemed old for his age, for childish games did not interest him much. Not that he was a sober grandfather of a lad—growing up in a small house crowded with brothers and sisters keeps anyone young, and he had a gay, teasing streak. Somewhere along the line, though, he took it for granted that he, not his father, had to bear responsibility for the whole family.

So he started out selling newspapers.

In the next three years, Muley made short stabs at three other careers. For a few weeks he worked for a local druggist, but pharmacy odors had nowhere near the appeal, for him, of pungent printer's ink. Then he ushered at Mayor Peter Staub's opera house, where traveling companies played "The Count of Monte Cristo," "Two Orphans," and other rip-snorting melodramas, and he made a little extra money selling candy in the intermission. Finally he let himself be convinced to try a stint in the grocery trade.

"This is a great opportunity for you, Adolph," his father told him, and somehow scraped together enough money for a train ticket to Providence, Rhode Island, where an uncle kept a prospering food store. The plan was for Muley to work days as a cash boy and go to business school at night.

Muley had his doubts right from the start. What fun would it be just saying, "Yes, Ma'am, thank you, Ma'am," all day? While the train ride was really special, living so far off with people who were practically strangers, was not.

Once in Rhode Island, he put his quick mind to the task of mastering storekeeping practice, and he learned the fundamentals of business bookkeeping. He also showed a hint of bold enterprise when a big political parade tooted through downtown Providence on a hot afternoon, headed for a flag-draped square where speeches galore were scheduled.

"There'll be a lot of thirsty people in that square," Muley told his uncle.

He coaxed a large basket of oranges and lemons from the store stock, made juice by hand—and later did a landoffice business selling orangeade and lemonade, netting a splendid profit of six dollars.

But homesickness conquered him in a few months, homesickness for his big, noisy, happy family and for the musty, ink-smeared Knoxville *Chronicle* office. At fourteen, he returned to Water Street, and from that age he never swerved again in his devotion to the newspaper profession.

Between his flyers into other fields, he had kept steadily at his paper delivery route and he resumed that job now. Although the endless walking was not particularly interesting, he loved the few tense minutes every dawn beside the clattery press, the wonderfully mysterious cases of metal type, the sharp, exciting ink smell in the air.

In school he heard about the great Horace Greeley, who had risen from barefoot New Hampshire farm boy to publisher of New York's famous *Tribune*. Then why not Muley Ochs? He would not have been his father's son if daydreams about someday owning a world-famous newspaper himself had not flashed through his head as he stood beside the noisy press.

But Muley was his mother's son, too. At dawn one autumn morning in 1872 he made up his mind to do something besides dream, and that same afternoon he marched into the front entrance of the Knoxville *Chronicle* office. He had jammed a cap on his unruly black curls to try to look more manly, but he was short for his age and wire-thin. Captain William Rule, the paper's publisher, stared in surprise as the slight, solemn boy asked him for a real newspaper job.

"What do you think you could do around here, bub?" the publisher asked with honest curiosity. Since his own work was long over when the press began slapping out papers for the carrier boys, Captain Rule did not recognize young Ochs as already a reliable employee.

Muley studied the dusty office with its litter of old papers, and grinned at the notion that even Horace Greeley could hardly have started with a better chance for showing one sort of skill. "I could sweep up some, for a start," he said.

The publisher leaned back in his creaky chair and laughed heartily. "You're on, bub," he said. Still chuckling, he added, "I believe there's a broom somewhere, back in the print shop."

Muley got the broom and eagerly set to work, sweeping, dusting, trimming the wick of the desk lamp. He made neat piles of old newspapers and he tidied the stack of books.

A few hours later, Captain Rule put down his scratchy quill pen, looked over his transformed office and agreed to pay his new helper $1.50 a week to keep the place clean—

the same $1.50 he had been getting for delivering newspapers. Muley's blue eyes shone as he hurried home, strutting like a peacock. Hadn't he watched a real publisher working? He had listened as a few paid advertisements were delivered by local merchants, eavesdropped while Captain Rule and his visitors exchanged the fascinating gossip there always is in any newspaper office. Now he was actually starting to learn about the newspaper business!

And that was exactly what he wanted to be doing. Right out in the street, Muley danced a little jig then jammed his cap on tight again and ran the rest of the way home.

Within a few months, his industry as an office boy impressed his boss so much that Captain Rule promoted him. His new job was that of printer's devil—traditionally the jack-of-all-trades printer's helper who cleans the press roller, races to the telegraph office to pick up late messages, wheels trays of type about the shop, darts out at all hours for beer and sandwiches.

"Muley" turned into "Ochsie" then, a new nickname given him by the noisy, hard-drinking, friendly printers for whom he slaved.

To take his new job, Ochsie quit school forever, a few months after his fifteenth birthday. He didn't feel he was learning too much there—and he may have been right. A composition he wrote at this period started:

> The E.T.U. [his school] is situated at knoxville, east tenn, it is situated on a hill in the northeastern part of knoxville, the government made an appropation to the University, & sent a U.S. Army Office there; since then it has become a military school, Now to go back to my subject...

He would learn more at the *Chronicle* than in school, he insisted to his parents, who were saddened by his decision. To them it meant the end of all hope of his attaining any sort of worldly success, and for days they went about shaking their heads gloomily. But their boy had never been happier.

Working hours were longer in those days than they are now, but the young printer's devil was free to leave by half-past eleven at night, after the type for the next morning's newspaper was locked in page forms ready for the press. Ochsie, however, chose to stay on later.

"I just don't like coming by the cemetery around midnight," he told his parents. Like any other boy brought up in the South then, he had heard a lot about how gravestones open at this witching hour, and, truthfully, he did not feel comfortable about being in the area then.

But he had another compelling reason, too. Walrus-moustached Henry Clay Collins, the press and printing foreman, liked him, he could tell. Mr. Collins had no objection to letting him fiddle around with extra type after the paper was locked up for the night. What's more, Mr. Collins lived only a hop and a skip from the Ochses, and he amiably welcomed the company of his young devil when he himself was ready to walk home around two in the morning.

So Ochsie waited—and while he waited, he tried a little typesetting. "No, Ochsie, old boy, you do it this way," Mr. Collins admonished while he instructed, and soon the lad learned how to set type by hand.

With deft fingers every letter of every word in the newspaper had to be painstakingly lifted from a type case. It took a great deal of dexterity to pick the proper metal letters quickly, then set them in the proper order in the frames that would fit onto the press.

Back then, before the days of linotype machines, let alone computers, setting type was a laborious business. The experienced typesetter, called a printer, could always get a job. By being at the *Chronicle* two extra hours every morning, Adolph Ochs learned enough before his sixteenth birthday to qualify for a new job as a full-fledged printer.

"You're all right, Ochsie!" Mr. Collins told him when he promoted him. "One of these days you'll have my job." But Mr. Collins's job was safe. Ochsie was dreaming of bigger worlds to conquer.

"I'm going to have a paper of my own someday," he told Mr. Collins calmly, and the foreman raised his bushy eyebrows a little. He was used to bold talk from printers, talk which usually came to nothing. Still, there was something out of the ordinary about Ochsie. Who could tell? He might be the one to do it.

In his own mind, Adolph was not only sure that he would someday be a publisher, but he was also clear about the kind of paper he wanted. It would be a big newspaper, big in size and in its ambitions, for it would print every scrap of news that would really help people make up their minds about important matters. And it would be a fair newspaper; it would print BOTH sides of every question.

How would a half-educated youth in the cultural backwater of Knoxville come to think of such inspired common sense?

No doubt part of the credit must go to his upright father, who loved, after dinner, to sit with his family and discuss great moral issues. Part must go, too, to the presence of a rich variety of vicious papers in the Reconstruction South. All over the country then, most newspapers were little more than opinionated propaganda sheets, for this was the heyday of venomous personal journalism and many publishers used their presses mainly to spread insults about their political enemies. But nowhere was the level lower than in Knoxville itself, where Parson William G. Brownlow's *Whig and Rebel Ventilator* held sway for years, abusing anyone who dared to disagree with the demagogic parson-politician.

Decent opinion even then deplored the Brownlow excesses. But the idea that a newspaper had a duty to print fair stories about its political enemies as well as its friends was not widely entertained. Somehow, at a very early age, Adolph Ochs came to entertain it.

Although he admired Captain Rule of the *Chronicle* and was to remain a close friend of his first boss for the rest of his life, his ambition already soared higher than a safe job on the captain's undistinguished daily. So after almost two years as a printer, Ochsie announced that he planned to quit.

He would strike out first for Louisville, he told his startled family. There Henry Watterson's *Courier-Journal* had made a great name as one of the Southland's leading newspapers, and he rather thought he could learn much by working for Marse Henry.

After that he might make his way to California as a printer. This was the great age of the tramp printer, the competent but usually unstable and often drunk printer who wandered from town to town, always sure of a newspaper berth because of his typesetting skill, but too fidgety to stay put in any one town for long.

Adolph Ochs had nothing of the tramp about him. In fact, he stuck out like a solemn, curly-haired little brother among the *Chronicle*'s easygoing, hard-drinking printers. However, now that he felt at home with them, he could shout out a song with the best, and pay back at least some of the rough teasing he got about his newly sprouting black moustache.

He was no tramp, but he had a giddy dream. If he could work his way out to California, where gold was making fortunes right and left, it might make his fortune, too. With a bagful of gold dust, he could ease the still difficult financial situation at home and have enough left over to start an honest little paper of his own somewhere.

Late one night in October of 1875, the whole staff of the *Chronicle*, from Captain Rule down, stayed to wish Ochsie Godspeed.

His successor as printer's devil brought oysters, beer and crackers from Mick's saloon up the street, and boards were set across type cases to make banquet tables. Then there were speeches as the beer flowed, increasingly flowery speeches about the grand future in store for Ochsie.

Finally, walrus-moustached Mr. Collins rose to offer his own tribute. "He is to a foreman what money is to a miser—a necessity hard to part with." Then for a going-away present, he handed Ochsie a small leather book, *The Poems of Thomas Hood*, with the names of all present waveringly scrawled on the flyleaf. Ochsie gulped hard to keep from bawling like a baby, and he was relieved when the party broke into boisterous song. Soon he was singing along with the rest, off-key but good and loud.

Even in the pages of the *Chronicle* the young printer's departure was noted. Captain Rule wrote in the October 13 edition:

> Mr. Adolph Ochs, for some years past an attaché of the *Chronicle* office, leaves on the westbound train today, on a protracted visit to Louisville, Ky. and other points.
>
> Mr. Ochs carries with him the well wishes of all connected with this office, and we would recommend him to all with whom he may come in contact, as a young man well worthy of their confidence and esteem.

With this glowing reference, Adolph S. Ochs set out into the world five months before his eighteenth birthday.

3

Getting a job on the Louisville *Courier-Journal* was easy. Armed with Captain Rule's editorial and an equally kind letter of introduction, Adolph had no trouble landing a printer's berth on the paper.

He worked quickly, quietly, and while his sure fingers sorted type his mind soaked up new ideas about how things were done on this lively, thriving daily. One skill escaped him, though; try as he would, he simply could not coax music from the little piccolo he had brought along from home. Finally a fellow printer, somewhat shaken by his shrill squeaking, offered to buy it. "It's no good," young Ochs warned. The printer took it and immediately blew a melodious trill. "I don't understand it," Ochsie said. "It wouldn't sing like that for me." But if he failed musically, he succeeded with a startling swiftness at his main endeavor. Within a month, he was promoted to assistant foreman of the composing room, the printers' domain on a big paper like the *Courier-Journal*.

Everybody liked the new young boss with the new moustache. "He's not a cheeky lad," older printers said. "He's willing to listen and learn. And he's a quick one." But Adolph felt restless, dissatisfied. He missed his family sorely; he longed to get on with his fortune hunt so he could help them, and then start that dream newspaper of his.

Instead of sleeping longer after working late at night, he wandered into the *Courier-Journal* newsroom in the morning when assignments were handed out. A babe in the woods here, he looked with awe at dapper editors and writers and decided he had to learn their trade, too, if he was ever going to run a newspaper. So he boldly asked for a chance.

"You might try copying a couple of bad debt cases down at the courthouse," the city editor said doubtfully. This skinny young printer in the mended suit did not inspire confidence. But soon the city editor began counting on young Ochs as a sound fellow. He was quick at routine jobs like copying cases from court records, and he went to a lot of trouble to get names spelled right if a runaway horse hurt some women out shopping. True, he was no great shakes at colorful writing, but you could trust his facts.

To save as much money as possible, Adolph stayed in Louisville with his cousins, the Francks. Lucien Franck, a young man about his own age, took on the task of keeping him from an all-work-and-no-play routine.

"There's going to be a party on Saturday evening," Lucien would say. "I promise you'll find some very pretty girls there."

"*Very* pretty?" Dolph, as Adolph was now called, would tease him. "In that case, I'll certainly come." He was a serious young man but at a party he sparkled, paid courtly compliments right and left, and danced with gusto. Still, at this point in his life he felt he could not afford much time or money for amusement.

"How much *do* you have in the bank, Dolph?" Lucien pressed him good-naturedly one evening. "You could stand at least one ticket to the play tonight."

Dolph's face suddenly turned grave. "I don't have a cent, Lu," he said, and passed him a letter from Knoxville.

". . . I am ashamed to send the children to school now," his mother had written. "They have no decent shoes and no stockings, and their clothes are almost past mending . . ." The letter had come earlier in the day, and Dolph had drawn his total savings of fifty-six dollars out of the bank and sent the money home.

Then, within a very few weeks, despite his own great plans and the progress he seemed to be making in Louisville, he himself followed the same route. If his family was having trouble, his place was with them. Giving up his giddy dream of California gold dust, a miserably homesick eighteen-year-old hurried back to Water Street.

This time it was to the Knoxville *Tribune* that he turned for a job as a printer. Going back to the *Chronicle* only six months after his brave farewell was probably too hard on his pride. But whatever the reason, the change proved fateful. Setting type at the *Tribune*, he met bearded Colonel John Encil MacGowan.

A gentleman old enough to be his father, the colonel had the same scholarly kindness as Captain Ochs. One difference stood out between the captain and the colonel, though: the latter had found a way to put his learning to use, writing newspaper editorials. He was one of the more gifted editorialists of his day.

This talented, experienced newspaperman and Adolph
became friends. At odd times during the day or evening, the
bearded man and the moustached youth sat in a corner, deep
in conversation. To the colonel's sympathetic ears, Adolph
poured out his dreams about running a new kind of newspaper. Other men might have laughed at the presumption of
the lad, but the colonel listened intently.

"You're on the right track," he said thoughtfully.

Joining this unlikely twosome now and again was the
Tribune's business manager, Franc Paul, a rolling stone of a
Tennessee newspaperman. Paul was one of the optimists
who kept the total of southern newspapers in a constant state
of flux, by bustling about the countryside buying failing
dailies or starting new ones.

When one of his own journalistic infants floundered, he
always managed to land back on his feet with a job on an
established paper. When he accumulated a little cash again,
he was ready for another stab at publishing. Now Paul had a
few hundred dollars saved up, and he began talking business
to Colonel MacGowan.

"I know the Chattanooga *Dispatch* can be bought cheap.
Will you come in on it with me?" he asked the colonel.

"Yes," MacGowan said. "But I want young Ochs with us."

Adolph leaped at the chance. He had no money to put
into the venture, of course. Enthusiasm, energy, his nimble
printer's fingers would be his contribution. Despite his parents' gloom at the prospect of his leaving home again, his
blue eyes gleamed. Perhaps everything had worked out for
the best. *This* would be his highroad to success!

On the first of April in 1877, Adolph Ochs, Colonel MacGowan and Franc Paul stepped off a steamboat onto a splintery wood pier where the Tennessee River takes its great westward bend at Chattanooga. They had come only a little more than a hundred miles down the river, but they were in another world.

Knoxville had suffered during the Civil War, but its suffering couldn't compare with what had happened to Chattanooga. Great armies had holed in there for long sieges, great battles like Chickamauga had been fought near by, and only a grim, ruined village had survived the war.

Then strong men who had spent long months in the shadow of magnificent Lookout Mountain during the war came back because they saw Chattanooga as a great natural river and railroad trading center. Others came when they heard rumors of iron ore in the mountains. Soon plank sidewalks stretched along muddy streets; shacks and stores sprang up; the smoke from an iron foundry rose above a booming settlement. Chattanooga in the 1870's had the rousing, raw newness of a western frontier town, complete even to rowdy saloons and pistol-packing characters galloping on the streets.

Adolph Ochs was entranced. His heart pounded at the thought of being a part of all this excitement, of being one of the powers on a real newspaper in a real city like this. On his mother's birthday, he wrote a letter to her in which his boyish glee shone through his pompous prose:

> May God spare you to see Nannie [his sister] married to a millionaire; George [his brother] President of the United States; Milton [another brother] a Senator; Ada [another sister] a famous author; and Mattie [another sister] a successful merchant or a large-salaried Rabbi's wife. As to

myself, my prayer is that I may soon be able to make for you all a comfortable home where want is unknown and send my brothers and sisters on their different roads rejoicing.

On this lively frontier city the Ochs-MacGowan-Paul trio made only the faintest impression. They divided up the responsibility for running their *Dispatch*, but three bosses were as bad as no boss. Nobody had the authority to make a sharp, quick decision and within a few months, the *Dispatch* ran completely out of money, and died.

The collapse of the paper left Adolph Ochs, at nineteen, marooned, penniless, far from home. He did not even have the price of a river steamer ticket back to Knoxville.

"I'll pay our debts," he promised MacGowan and Paul. "Let me have use of the *Dispatch* press, and I'll look for small printing jobs."

A rickety affair with not many months of life left to it, this press was the only asset the partners still owned. The two older men took young Ochs at his word; they let him have the press, while they sought greener fields elsewhere, and he kept his part of the bargain. Soon he had paid back every penny of their common debt. What's more, while roaming the board sidewalks in quest of printing clients, Adolph got an idea.

There were no telephones then, or telephone directories. When a new person in town wanted to find a blacksmith or a banker, he asked around. But Chattanooga was growing too big for this word-of-mouth system. Adolph decided to compile a city directory for growing Chattanooga.

In between grinding out small printing orders, he trudged up and down every street in town, painstakingly jotting notes. He introduced himself to every businessman, told about his directory plan, asked questions. When he appeared, many a solid citizen smiled at the big words used by this slight, unprepossessing youth. Still boyishly skinny, only five feet and seven inches tall, he cut less than a commanding figure. But he talked great good sense.

Certainly a city directory would be a wonderful help for the business community, every merchant agreed. This young Ochs had a good head on his shoulders. But did he have the talent to follow through?

The fact that he was Jewish had no bearing in the melting pot that Chattanooga was then. With just about every shade of religious doctrine represented, casual tolerance was the rule. If a man could do a job, nobody cared much where he came from or where he worshipped. With the publication of his 126-page directory, Adolph Ochs proved to the people who were most important that he could do a hard job well.

All by himself, he had carried out what amounted to a census—and then he printed a book that later became a gold mine for local historians.

Its statistics showed that Chattanooga late in 1877 had 11,448 residents, compared to less than 2,000 in 1865—a leap of almost 600 per cent in only twelve years. The local population was gloriously varied: only 773 citizens out of the 11,448 had been born in the state of Tennessee, and the rest had come either from thirty-two other states (of the thirty-eight then in the Union, only California, Colorado, Nebraska, Nevada and Vermont were not represented) or else from sixteen different foreign countries (Austria, Canada, Cuba, Denmark, England, France, Germany, Holland, Hungary, Italy, Mexico, Norway, Russia, Scotland, Sweden and

Switzerland). And there were three children who fit none of these categories, for they had been born at sea.

The directory also disclosed that Chattanooga had nineteen metal-working shops, sixteen wood-working concerns, two carriage and wagon makers, three brick kilns, three flour mills, two textile mills and an ice manufacturer. And it was home port for ten steamships, besides countless barges.

Wonderfully useful though this directory was in its own day, it did not make Adolph's fortune. The few hundred dollars it brought in had to pay a printing bill after all, for the wheezy old *Dispatch* press had collapsed. What profit remained just about kept the young publisher in food and lodging for a few months.

Right after his directory appeared, he merely marked time, managing to exist on his sparse profit, eking out a few more dollars with odd printing jobs, sending two or three dollars to Knoxville every week. But he knew what he was waiting for. In his wanderings around town, he had heard that the only real newspaper in town, the *Times*, was having hard sledding. The owner would surely be wanting to get rid of it soon. If so, this unpromising four-page daily would be his passport to the estate of publisher! Finally, with a thrill of triumph, he heard that the Chattanooga *Times* was for sale.

The paper was typical of its time and place, and had already had three or four different owners in its nine years of existence. It could claim no journalistic distinction; it was selling barely 250 copies a day; its assets amounted to little more than its flimsy press in a wreck of a building at Eighth and Cherry streets.

Yet to Adolph Ochs this was a grand and glorious opportunity for putting his dream to the test.

From his experience on the ill-fated *Dispatch*, he had salvaged one lesson he would never forget—that to run a newspaper the way he thought it should be run, he would have to have absolute control. Older, possibly wiser men had failed to make a go of the *Times*, but no matter. He had to take the chance. His head was full of ideas for covering all the news, printing it neatly, making a paper any solid citizen would have to read. All by himself, he had to raise the money to buy the *Times*.

He had no magic lamp to rub, no wondrous genie to help him. Completely on his own, a few months after his twentieth birthday, he proceeded to bargain with S. A. Cunningham, editor and owner of the *Times,* who was desperate to sell. First Cunningham asked $800 in cash. Then he reduced the price to $250 in cash for a half-interest in the paper—the other half to be sold in two years at a sum to be agreed upon by impartial arbitrators. However, full authority over the paper would go to the new owner after the first payment.

Adolph Ochs marched into the First National Bank of Chattanooga. He had no account at the bank; he had no money in any bank. He owned no property at all that might guarantee a loan.

"I need some money," he said calmly.

The bank officer he spoke to was sympathetic, for this was one of the men Ochs had impressed during the directory days. Still, the cautious approach of the proper banker prevailed—at first.

"I'd like to give you some cash," the banker said. "I think you're a good risk. But we would have to have someone in town endorse the loan for you—to guarantee the money."

"There's no one here in town who knows me any better than you do," Ochs said firmly.

The banker sat back and thought hard a minute. "I guess you're right," he said, and he signed the endorsement for a $300 loan.

Adolph then got in touch with Colonel MacGowan. Forty-seven years old, a man of experience and talent, the colonel, too, took a chance on his twenty-year-old friend. He agreed to work as editor-in-chief of the *Times*. There would be only the wildly inadequate sum of $50 left in the new publisher's pocket after he paid off Cunningham, so Colonel MacGowan set his own salary at $1.50 a day for the time being. And four printers stranded by the death of the *Dispatch* signed on, too. With less than $3 in cash among them, they were willing to work awhile for short pay.

Now Ochs hurried up and down the walks of Chattanooga from early morning to midnight, trying to charm merchants into promising ads after the paper changed hands. "Help me," he pleaded. "You'll see, the *Times* will be the kind of paper that will help you." He was busy every second, almost too busy to think, but when his head touched his pillow late at night, he marveled at the thought that soon he would be the owner of an honest to goodness newspaper.

On July 1, 1878, less than nine years from the day a barefoot boy in Knoxville began delivering newspapers, control of the Chattanooga *Times* officially passed into the hands of Adolph S. Ochs. For the formal payment ceremony, his father came down from Knoxville, not just for sentimental reasons, but because his son could not yet sign legal papers. He was eight months short of his twenty-first birthday!

4

On the front page of the Chattanooga *Times* of July 2, 1878, one item told about a "big baseball match this afternoon between the Roanoke Iron Company team and the Little Jokers, admission, 15¢." Another item read: "The hop at the Natural Bridge House, Lookout Mountain, to-night, will be an elegant affair. Mr. Thomas will have a splendid string band and Japanese lanterns will illuminate the grounds." Mixed with the jumble of short local and telegraph items, the reader could also find: "Should times be called depressingly hard when people of a city the size, and containing the wealth, of Chattanooga raise $1,500 for a Fourth of July frolic?"

By far the most prominent display on the front page went to a two-column ad shouting: "THE BEST SHIRT for $1, Equal to any sold in the city for $1.25. FANS! FANS! FANS! Handsome and cheap. Embroideries down! down! down!"

But the most significant words in the paper appeared under the masthead on the editorial page—"Adolph S. Ochs, Publisher."

Directly below this was the statement of policy that custom demanded of every new publisher. Probably few people bothered reading every word, for new publishers came and went with the seasons in Chattanooga. And in the style of the time, the statement ran to more than five hundred words of less than sparkling prose. Still, Ochs had improved as a writer since his school days. He began:

> It will be the foremost purpose of the manager of this newspaper to make it the indispensable organ of the business, commercial and productive, of Chattanooga, and of the mineral and agricultural districts of Tennessee, North Georgia and Alabama.
>
> The paper will contain the latest news by telegraph, markets from all the leading centers of trade, and the freshest news by mail. The local news department shall be as near perfect as hard work and vigilance can make it. In the items of general, commercial and local information, it is proposed to leave nothing to be desired, and no room for home or foreign competition. . . .

But nowhere in all this forest of words was the stock, fervent pledge to beat the drums ceaselessly for a particular politician or political cause. This was by far the most notable thing about his statement. As something of a sop to prevailing opinion then, Ochs did write that his newspaper would "move in line with the Conservative Democracy of the South." That he would stand for no name-calling or news-slanting he did not say.

But lofty aims were all very well. From the instant he took control of the *Times*, Ochs found himself facing harsh, practical problems. If his great newspaper dream was not to evaporate into mist, he had to move fast.

On his first day in control, he discovered a bill that positively had to be paid. The Associated Press in New York, which was the paper's main supplier of news beyond Chattanooga's limits, wired a threat to cut off all telegrams if payment for the service was not sent at once. The *Times* was "in bad odor," it said; no credit whatsoever would be extended to such a shaky proposition. The only money Ochs had in the world at that point was $37.50, left from the bank's $300 after paying $250 to Cunningham and $12.50 in legal fees in connection with signing the contract. He sent $25 to the AP, leaving himself with a total working capital of $12.50.

Adolph Ochs was no fool. He knew it took cash to run any sort of business. But with a calm to be envied by the boldest poker player, he proceeded to run his newspaper—despite the nightmare risk involved. If he failed, if the paper collapsed and he was left owing money right and left, his name could be ruined; probably never again would older men, or any men, trust him. Still he plunged ahead, for he had faith that he *could not* fail.

Every penny had to be spent where it would do the most good. His July 3 record read: "one lamp chimney, 5¢; man to carry oil, 5¢; lead pencils 10¢ . . ."

Meeting his payroll at the end of the week was out of the question, even though Colonel MacGowan and the printers had to eat. The paper supply was running low, and at the end of the month there would be rent to pay, a whole $24 for the creaky old building. And if the *Times* was to attract readers, at least a few new cases of type would have to be bought somehow; much of the type he had inherited was so worn that it would not print a clear impression.

These pressures drove Ochs ceaselessly. No circus juggler was more agile than he at this period. Mornings he rushed to call on a dozen merchants, pleaded for ads, and then took handwritten slips redeemable for groceries or cloth, as payment for the ads. At the end of a week, he passed these slips out to his staff instead of money. Cash was scarce throughout the area, and this barter system worked reasonably well, but it took a fearful toll of the young publisher's energy.

To meet some bills, though, he needed money. The *Times* had a horrible financial reputation because of its poor record in the past; it was "in bad odor" with a lot of firms besides the Associated Press. Ochs worked out a system of his own for dealing with suspicious creditors.

When the rent came due, he briskly took the bill from the dubious landlord.

"You will have your check tomorrow," Ochs said. "It is our policy to audit all bills before paying them."

Somehow he made this sound reasonable to the landlord, and then the next day a check was really ready—not an ordinary check, but a most ornate, imposing-looking check printed on the paper's press. This made an impression of solid respectability on the landlord, and so did the fact that the bank honored the check by paying out cash for it.

What the landlord and the other creditors did not know about was the frantic borrowing Ochs had managed to do overnight. To pay one man, he borrowed from another, and deposited money in his bank account barely in time to make sure his ornate check would be honored.

A man tinged even slightly with dishonesty would have tripped up on a regime like this. More than once, Adolph skated perilously close to the line, but somehow he always managed to get the money to back his checks, and soon creditors stopped pressing him so closely. They would let him wait till the end of the month to meet his bills. His system had served its purpose.

Whatever energy he had left, he put into improving the newspaper. He bought a few cases of clearer type to make the *Times* easier to read. He designed a neater front page. He blue-penciled gossip and featured hard news. But this was a slow, undramatic process. It took time for the stamp of his personality to show up, and he almost lost the time he needed when, over and above his own problems, disaster struck Chattanooga. Late in the summer of 1878 an epidemic of yellow fever broke out.

With the first hot weather that year, the dreaded Yellow Jack had appeared in New Orleans. The killing fever traveled relentlessly up the Mississippi valley during June and July. Chattanooga, miles to the east and sheltered by its mountains, charitably raised money for the aid of victims elsewhere. The *Times* carried stories about a ball for the benefit of the less fortunate far away, and ladies baked cakes to sell for the cause. Refugees fleeing from stricken towns were cautiously welcomed.

Then in August, one of these refugees in Chattanooga came down with "pernicious bilious fever." That was all that was wrong with him, people insisted at first. Then another family got sick; the first man weakened, turned lemon-yellow and died. There could be no more mincing of words now. Yellow fever had hit the city! Panic started early in September.

By river boat, by cart, on foot, hundreds of families fled. Terrified communities up and down the river refused to let boats from Chattanooga stop at their landings. Emergency tent cities sprang up in the hills. Chattanooga's Board of Health helped some of the frightened families wait out the epidemic by establishing a camp in the wilderness near Blowing Springs, Georgia. But more than that the Board of Health could not do in those pre-vaccination days. The cause of yellow fever was not known, let alone the means for preventing it. People knew only that it flourished in hot, steamy climates. Twenty years later Dr. Walter Reed of the United States Army discovered that the bite of a swamp mosquito brought on the dread sickness. Mosquito-breeding swamps were drained, all but wiping out the disease, and a vaccine was developed to protect possible victims.

But in Chattanooga in 1878, all people could do was vaguely blame the fever on a mysterious poison in the air. To admit that your city had some of this poison was to insult its fair name. By September, however, there could no longer be any doubt of the poison in Chattanooga's air.

Its wooden sidewalks were deserted. Almost all business stopped. Chattanooga boats seeking only to buy food for the afflicted city were turned back at other towns. But the compassionate from as far away as New York City and even Paris, France, sent money. Brave doctors came from Mississippi and Atlanta.

The onset of the epidemic had caught Ochs out of Chattanooga. His frantic quest for money had driven him to seek loans in other cities. The custom of the day was for railroads to give free passes to newspaper owners, and he had used his to ride as far as Cincinnati on a wild chance that he could raise some cash there. He tried Louisville and Knoxville, too. In Knoxville, joyously visiting with his family and getting reacquainted with his fantastically grown brothers and sisters, he got the news about Yellow Jack.

"Don't go back, Dolph," his mother begged. "Stay home. Your place is here."

"I have to go back, Ma," he insisted. "The paper can't quit."

Colonel MacCowan wired, adding his own plea that Ochs could do more good away from Chattanooga for the time being. "The fewer people here, the quicker we can lick Bronze John," MacGowan said.

His mother and MacGowan convinced him, but he foresaw a more pressing need for money than ever before. When the epidemic was over, cash would be incredibly scarce in Chattanooga, and if the *Times* was to continue, he would have to have some money in reserve. So he spent the next anxious weeks trying to raise cash in the South.

Meanwhile, Colonel MacGowan stayed on the job. So did peppery, red-bearded Will Kennedy, who had recently been hired as the paper's sole reporter, and so did a few of the printers. Between them, they put out a one-page newspaper every single day, a heroic, heart-breaking record of a city's existence under siege.

Police, undertakers, ministers, doctors and nurses stayed, too. Pausing in their terrible rounds, they read Will Kennedy's quips, and smiled. "The hospital is awful handy to the graveyard," he wrote on the ninth of October. "Eleven deaths yesterday, and more coming. Trot out your next funeral."

Although nobody knew what had caused the outbreak of fever, everybody knew that cold weather would halt its deadly march. Every prayer was for frost. On Halloween night there was a light frost, and the next morning, for the first time in more than a month, the regular westbound train of the Western and Atlantic Railroad stopped at the Chattanooga station. Then on the night of the sixth of November, there was a hard frost. The peril was past!

In two months, Yellow Jack had taken 366 lives in Chattanooga. Losses to local merchants were put at half a million dollars, a staggering sum for a community its size in a day when the dollar went much further than it does today. As for the Chattanooga *Times*, it came out of the dreadful two months with a debt of $600.

Early in November, when Ochs was back in town, calm and confident despite every trial, he wrote an editorial titled "Our Plague," in which he said: "Will this ruin Chattanooga? No! If this city was born to be ruined, it would have been blotted out years ago."

With the drag of urgent debts, and against every dictate of sober common sense, Adolph Ochs plunged ahead to build up his newspaper and his adopted city.

One of his first steps was to seek out better quarters for the *Times*. Printing a clear, readable newspaper in its present plant could not be done, so he rented a bigger place down the block. By no means a palace, this was only a couple of rooms above McCorkle's Saloon and Bowling Alley, but at least there was space for a better press. He had no money to pay for this; he borrowed and borrowed some more.

He was not content to just squeak by, instead he followed his instinct. Not only did he want a newspaper; he wanted a *good* newspaper. With steady nerves, he gambled on success.

Some notes he jotted down around this period give an idea of the financial contortions he was going through: "Jan. 3, borrowed $300 from First National; Jan. 4, H. H. Suder paid me $108, a Godsend; borrowed from Ewing Brothers $125 for a few days; asked Mr. Z. C. Patten for the loan of $200 for a few days but he could not do it, he was going to the bank to try to get some for himself."

And then, nothing daunted: "Jan. 6, borrowed of Moon and McMillin, to be returned Monday, $100; Jan. 14, Father overdrew $192 at bank, but had deposited $150 he had borrowed from D.B.L. and Company to be returned today, endorsed a renewal of $100 for sixty days for Colonel MacGowan . . ."

The reference to "Father" did mean Captain Ochs. At Dolph's urging, the captain had moved his family down to Chattanooga so they could all be together again. What's more, the captain had come to work for his son, as treasurer of the paper, a post he filled with patience and real ability.

Besides directing all of this financial juggling, Adolph Ochs also kept a finger on every aspect of the newspaper's operation. He didn't write very much, leaving that mostly to the competent colonel and Will Kennedy. But any hour of the day or night, he was likely to be busy searching out ads for the paper, changing a headline in the composing room, suggesting an idea for a story. "Do you think it would be a good idea . . ." he would say gently, and nobody on his staff minded listening, for he was always willing to listen, too.

But with so much of the mature man about him, he still kept a little boyish touch or two. When his twenty-first birthday rolled around in March, he could not resist picking up a quill pen himself and writing an editorial which he titled: "A Specimen of a Newspaperman's Cheek Blowing His Own Horn."

We do not regard it as necessary to make any apologies for the remarks that follow. We are but human, and have our full share of self-admiration. This is a happy day with the publisher of this paper, and it is almost impossible to keep our happiness out of these columns. Though born in Cincinnati, Ohio, we have not until today become a citizen. Our happiness comes from the fact that today we are 21 years of age and have become a citizen—a man. Long have we looked to the time when we would have attained our majority, and many have been the bright pictures we have fancied ourselves the center of at this time. How many of these hopes have been realized we need not say.

We take this occasion to state that notwithstanding a *boy* has published the *Times* since last July; the *Times* has under his administration steadily increased in circulation and patronage, so that today we can boast that the *Times* has as large, if not a larger circulation than any paper in East Tennessee. We return our thanks to the citizens of Chattanooga and vicinity for the liberal encouragement given the present management of the *Times*, and we hope to merit a continuance of same.

Later that week, a *Times* reader sent in a letter which Ochs printed. "I must say," this reader wrote, "if the *Times* was being published by a boy since you became the purchaser, then I wish there were more 'boys.'"

5

Not long after the boy publisher rounded the turn into man's estate, his *Times* slowly but unmistakably began to make money. There was no way to pinpoint the exact moment when it became a profitable enterprise; the change came too gradually. But as the second anniversary of his purchase approached, the change in its status became clear—painfully clear.

Under his original agreement with Cunningham, arbitrators had to study his books after two years. Although Cunningham had handed over full direction of the paper in 1878 for $250, he had retained ownership of a half-interest. After two years, arbitrators were to set a fair price for this. In 1878, when the *Times* was not much of a newspaper, Cunningham had been willing to sell it outright for $800; but now, in 1880, after two years of Ochs management, the *Times* was healthy, growing, prospering. The arbitrators put the value of Cunningham's half-interest at a stunning $5,500— twenty-two times what half the paper had been worth two years earlier.

Ochs was staggered. To assume full legal ownership of the *Times*, he had to pay this. In effect, he would be handing out a total of $5,750 for a paper he could have bought only two years ago for $800, but there was no help for it. However, he had learned a lesson. Never again, he warned himself, never again sign a blind contract like that. He knew now that he should have tried even harder to raise the entire $800, and that if this had proved impossible he should have at the very least insisted back in '78 on setting a firm price for the second payment.

Now he had to get his hands on that much money. Glumly he trudged out on his borrowing rounds again; he *had* to have clear title to the *Times*. Now he was juggling loans in the thousands, not the hundreds, but his tactics were the same. His days were dogged by anxious creditors, his sleep disturbed by bank-note nightmares. Even his steady nerve faltered now and then. On New Year's Day in 1881, he wrote in his diary:

> Dismal day. Seems as if the new year is not to be a good one for me. How to wash out of financial troubles bothers me. Prospects gloomy. I have thought of many plans, but the next few days must tell what I shall do. My entire indebtedness will be no less than $9,000, all of it due within the next two years.

But now bankers were more willing to lend him money. Gradually he was able to pull himself out of his financial crisis, because he had a vigorous, popular newspaper as solid evidence of his good judgment. He was also putting out a farmers' weekly as a side line, and this was making money. But the real reason why loans were easier to get was because of the *Times* itself.

Apart from its money-making power, it had turned into a good newspaper—an excellent one for its time. Ochs had made the paper more attractive-looking; he printed all the straight, unbiased news he could get; he played fair with advertisers, neither giving nor receiving any special favors. The *Times* had more news than any other paper, and its news could be trusted. To Chattanoogans of the 1880's, the *Times* stood head and shoulders above any competition.

Moreover, the *Times* was intelligently edited. When thoughtful doctors suggested that open sewers and stagnant puddles might have some connection with disease, Ochs had MacGowan campaign on the editorial page for better civic sanitation. Memory of the yellow fever epidemic still stirred the city. Ochs sensed that responsible citizens would welcome a newspaper with a high sense of journalistic responsibility on a matter like this.

No crusader, Ochs did not beat the bushes for fiery causes to support. In its opinion columns on the editorial page, the *Times* spoke up for more and better public schools, for a library, an opera house, a fireman's fountain, the dredging of a deeper channel in the Tennessee River, all worthy civic improvements that Ochs personally supported. His own thinking paralleled that of most solid citizens. Instinctively he knew what kind of newspaper they needed and liked.

He also shared the "booster" philosophy of his time. All patriotic citizens of Chattanooga hoped with all their hearts that their city was destined to become "the Pittsburgh of the South." It had railroads, iron, a great river. Surely in the next half-century it would become one of the industrial giants of America. Adolph Ochs believed this; with his energy and ambition, he would. And as a shrewd publisher, he saw that boosting Chattanooga could only help the Chattanooga *Times*.

So as the months passed, he managed to pay back every penny he owed. "Work hard and pay your debts," his father drummed at him. He did just that.

Now his father, surprisingly, was proving a real tower of strength at the *Times*. After floundering so often on his own, he turned out to have a gift for keeping accounts straight and conducting business affairs efficiently—as long as the plans were made by someone else. Working for his son did not sour him. The affection between the two was too strong for either of them to be troubled by this trick of fate. Morally the bearded captain still was unquestioned head of the family; financially his son Adolph was. Cash to put his younger brothers through college, which he already regretted missing, came from his coffers.

By 1882, when he was only twenty-four years old, Adolph Ochs had an enviable position. The respected owner of the best newspaper in town, he was sought after to serve on the school board and to lend his name to every worthy cause. Early in the year, he symbolized his standing as a community leader by buying a big, rambling brick house at the corner of Cedar and Fifth streets, one of the better residential areas of Chattanooga.

There his bustling mother cheerfully bossed her brood into eating well of her good home-cooking. Dolph began to put on a little weight. He no longer looked like a gawky boy, and now that he didn't have to rely on a bristly moustache to show his maturity he shaved it off. With his alert blue eyes, his strong and yet gentle face, his tamed shock of black hair, he had no trouble impressing the young ladies, and for the first time in his life he began to give serious thought to natty suits and cravats. He also began to think about finding a wife. Within a few months, when he was calling on a business acquaintance in Cincinnati, he found her.

The business friend was Leo Wise, son of Rabbi Isaac M. Wise, founder and president of Hebrew Union College, a man widely known for his scholarship and his wit. The leader of the reform branch of his faith, he was also a cherished friend of many distinguished men of other religions. Besides his son, he had a pretty daughter, Iphigene.

Waiting in the parlor for Leo, Adolph was startled by a slim, bright-eyed young woman who walked in and blithely announced: "I'm Effie Miriam Wise. Who are you?"

Ochs had a glib tongue with young women. He knew how to pay a courtly compliment and deliver a bouquet of posies with gallant manner. But suddenly his tongue stumbled over his own name.

Haltingly, he finally managed to introduce himself. Then, till Leo came down, he carried on a poor excuse for a conversation on the only subject he could think of somehow. In his confusion, he told this surprising girl about the horse race he had seen the day before, between a horse called Longfellow and another called Henry Bassett. These were famous racers of the day, true, but hardly an inspired subject for impressing a demure female.

Effie seemed amused at his embarrassment. "I love horses," she finally helped him. In his gratitude, he offered to send her a souvenir shoe of Henry Bassett's, which he had picked up after the race.

He had started off awkwardly, but he was determined to see Effie again. He found one excuse after another for coming up to Cincinnati, and he wore his free railroad pass to shreds. Effie listened with a faint smile as he poured out his plans for making his newspaper bigger and better. She liked to read books? Maybe she could write some notes about new books to put in the paper. She loved waltzing? Well, he did, too, and there was going to be a fine ball in Chattanooga after Thanksgiving. Would she do him the honor of coming and visiting then?

She came. She saw his newspaper office. Strolling sedately in her long, full skirt, she inspected every dusty inch of the composing room. She stayed with the big, cheerful Ochs family in their comfortable brick house on Cedar Street. She was a quiet, shy girl despite her lively eyes. The exuberance of the Ochses startled her at first. Adolph's bustling energy took away her breath—but his blue eyes were so gentle when he looked at her. Effie was conquered.

They were married on February 28, 1883, in the Plum Street Synagogue in Cincinnati. So happy that he wanted to shout his joy to the world, the young bridegroom hired a private railroad car for the occasion, to bring Chattanooga friends to the wedding.

Effie made a lovely bride. In the Cincinnati *Commercial-Gazette* of the next day, she was described as "a petite brunette of the most pronounced and brilliant type, with magnificent black eyes and level brows, and an extraordinary wealth of raven hair." Then the paper went on to say that "she has been highly educated and inherits much of her distinguished father's intellectual acumen, as well as that gaiety of temper and brilliant wit which makes him a most enjoyable companion."

For their honeymoon, Adolph took his bride to Washington, D.C. President Chester Arthur invited him and his wife to tea at the White House. The barefoot Knoxville boy had come a long way indeed.

On their return to Chattanooga, the young couple got a royal reception. Throughout March parties were held in their honor, and everybody who was anybody came to wish them happiness.

All of these fond wishes seemed to be coming true in the months that followed. Effie moved into the big brick house on Cedar Street, an arrangement that suited her perfectly, for the details of housekeeping had never interested her and she was delighted to let Dolph's mother fuss over him as always. Mrs. Ochs fussed over her, too, the way she did over her own daughters. Effie didn't mind a bit. Every evening when Dolph came home, he brought her flowers or some little trinket. Often she went back to the *Times* with him after dinner and sat at a desk carefully penning a book review while he read proofs in the composing room. In the spring he bought her a horse and even went on genteel morning rides with her.

Then sorrow struck. Effie's first child died at birth. A few years later, she and Dolph again had the unutterably sad experience of losing a baby. Seriously ill this time, Effie took months to recover. In time, she was writing her book reviews again and carrying on almost as usual, but she was left weakened and a prey to quiet melancholy. It seemed likely that she would never become a mother.

Even Adolph's optimism was shaken by this private sorrow. Always a sympathetic man, he became a compassionate man. Having known tragedy himself, he could feel more keenly for other people in great trouble.

A man has the consolation of his work, though, and with his driving energy Ochs could not give in to grief for long. He plunged back into a routine that would have exhausted any other man.

As always, he spent long hours at the *Times*. Now his brothers George and Milton had finished school and both had responsible jobs on the paper.

But running the newspaper, and keeping an eye on George and Milton, occupied only a part of Adolph Ochs's working day. Along with his *Times* concerns, he served a term on the school board. He took on a few other side-line business connections, as a director of a drug firm and of the Chattanooga Steamship Company. He chaired a committee formed to create a national park on the Chickamauga battlefield.

Whenever a civic cause cried out for energetic direction, Adolph lent his energy. His big house became a center for all sorts of civic gatherings. Whenever an eminent visitor came to Chattanooga, he was almost sure to be entertained on Cedar Street.

One visitor—President Grover Cleveland—did not dine on Cedar Street, but Ochs entertained him notably when he came to town for a few days. The unusual nature of the entertainment made the occasion memorable for both men.

Ochs had been assigned to a place in one of the first carriages of a parade planned to take the President through town, then up Lookout Mountain to the battle site. Ochs, who was becoming a bit of a dandy, felt he did not have the proper coat for the occasion. There was no time to buy one, so he borrowed a suitable gray coat from a cousin. Now he could ride in style directly in the President's eye.

But during the excursion, it began to rain. Adolph was in an open carriage that could not be closed. The seats were upholstered in a bright red plush, and the red of the plush, wet by the rain, began to run—right onto the seat of Ochs's elegant borrowed coat. When he stood up to shake the President's hand before the ensuing ceremony started, both men had a good laugh together about the sartorial mishap. Only the cousin was not amused.

Appeased by a new coat, the cousin teased Ochs about cutting a ridiculous figure before the President. But Ochs was not worried. In a few minutes of private conversation, he and President Cleveland had measured each other to their mutual satisfaction. President Cleveland had been favorably impressed, Ochs was sure.

But before their paths crossed again, Ochs had another busy decade in Chattanooga. It was a strange and wonderful time in the city's history—a crazy boom and bust time, marvelously exciting to the people living there.

The first electric lights had switched on in Chattanooga in 1882. New industry was cropping up all over town. Suddenly one man, then another, began to buy up empty lots that would make fine factory sites. Land was cheap still, and it was bound to zoom in value as the city expanded. And zoom it did, in the next few years, to twice, thrice, ten, a hundred times its former value as land-buying became the rage.

Anybody with a few spare dollars could play this fascinating game. Wasn't Chattanooga on its way to challenge Pittsburgh and Chicago? Even parcels of ground way out in the hills were snatched up as potential fortune-making home-sites.

Adolph Ochs, as whole-hearted a booster as Chattanooga had, printed glowing stories of plans for new development schemes. What if land prices were skyrocketing because of all the buying? Land had been absurdly cheap till now and prices were coming more in line with real value.

To his father, Ochs talked enthusiastically about one grand project after another. But somehow Captain Ochs could not catch the spark. In his own younger days, the captain would surely have been among the first to rush out and join the parade himself—and yet now he seemed uninterested.

While frenzied speculating went on all around him, the captain withdrew more and more to a quiet task he had set himself. As a guide for his children when he should be gone, he was writing the story of his life, filling page on page with his youthful travels and the morals he had drawn from all his ups and downs. It was almost as if he sensed his death was near.

For in the fall of 1888, shortly before reaching his sixtieth birthday, Captain Julius Ochs took sick and died. The grief his wife and children felt pushed all other considerations aside. Because he knew this would have pleased his father, Adolph gave him a military funeral, with a uniformed detachment of Union veterans marching beside the coffin and the sad notes of a bugler playing "Taps" sounding over his grave. Adolph's mother, who had never lost her loyalty to the Confederate cause, this once relaxed her stern convictions and approved of Dolph's decision.

The loss of his father would never cease to sadden him, but Adolph was too full of life and zest not to bounce back from the blow. Gradually, he resumed his busy schedule, lonelier but still full of plans. He spent long hours at his newspaper office, and he bustled to countless meetings where new development ideas were being discussed.

In his zeal, Ochs bought many parcels of land himself. He also took a leading part in the establishment of an incredible organization called the Chattanooga Land, Coal, Iron and Railway Company. This was formed by a group of ambitious citizens to buy up 20,000 acres of open land across the Tennessee River from Chattanooga, and construct what amounted to a new city, complete with industry, homes, a railroad. In popular talk, the syndicate planning all this was the "Over-the-River Company."

Among the owners of the land was a Mr. Hampton, skeptical about the whole deal. He refused to sell to a paper committee. However, since Adolph Ochs was mixed up in the project, he said, and since Ochs was a responsible man, he could buy the land, if he wanted it.

Such was the frenzy of the time that Ochs, for all his acute business sense, signed his name to a contract to buy Hampton's land for $103,000. The whole Over-the-River scheme would take about twelve million dollars, a fabulous sum for the day. The price of Hampton's tract seemed only a drop in the bucket.

But the land boom had just about run its course. When metal experts found there was too high a sulfur content in the iron ore around Chattanooga for it to make good steel, dreams of the city's challenge to Pittsburgh abruptly faded. Birmingham, Alabama, would be the South's heavy industry center, for its iron was purer, and Chattanooga would have to settle for lesser glory. Prices for parcels of land that might have been used for great foundries suddenly slumped. Just as swiftly as the boom had started, it collapsed.

The collapse put the Over-the-River Company out of business, and it left Adolph Ochs saddled with a personal debt of $103,000. From a moral point of view, the whole committee was responsible for paying this huge sum to Hampton. But Ochs alone was legally responsible because only his name had been signed to the contract. Hampton sued him for the money.

Ochs's lawyer pleaded in court that the purchase had been made in the name of the company, that other members of the group had actually taken part in the negotiations. To this, Hampton's lawyer replied that his client had a contract not with a bankrupt company but with a reputable citizen.

While his own lawyer was rising to protest again, Ochs stood up in court.

"Mr. Swaney," he said to Hampton's lawyer, "you have won your case." Other committee members, who were all hard pressed by the bursting of the financial bubble, offered sympathy but no cash. So Ochs sold everything he could— except his newspaper—and a few days later he delivered a check for $103,000 to the landowner whose suspicions had been only too quickly justified.

Ochs lost other money, too, in the bust after the land boom, but this one enormous loss was by far the hardest blow. And it came at a time when money was tight again, a time when he needed every dollar he could get, for Ochs was engaged in the most expensive undertaking of his career. He was building a great, new gold-domed home for his newspaper.

The new plant was to be among the South's grandest, of magnificent granite, a full six stories high. People had come for miles to watch the cornerstone ceremony. Now the building was about half finished, but completing it would cost tens of thousands—and after paying Hampton, Ochs was broke.

But it had to be finished.

Telling no one of his true financial plight, Adolph Ochs set out once more to borrow, borrow and borrow again.

6

Great granite blocks for the new Chattanooga *Times* building kept arriving at the wharves, and sturdy teams of horses dragged them up to the site. Rope-hoisting workmen unloaded them and lifted them higher and higher as the building rose above Chattanooga's rooftops. Construction lagged a bit, but it did not stop.

Ochs roamed as far as New York in his frantic search for cash to pay for all this. For two reasons, he would not borrow closer to home. In the first place, he was determined to keep his plight secret, to keep up a brave front of financial solidity; he dreaded seeing any lowering of his newspaper's prestige. Second, even if his pride hadn't stood in his way, he would have had trouble raising loans locally, for all Chattanooga was feeling a money pinch after the collapse of the land boom.

A man of some consequence in much of the South, Ochs still felt like a country boy in the big city up North. Writing home to

Effie, he listed a few of the "bright lights" he had met at a banquet of newspaper officials, and then added, as if amazed:

"I was introduced as one of the most successful newspaper publishers in the South. I spoke for a few minutes at the dinner. I don't quite remember what I said, but I was frequently applauded."

The boy who had dreamed grandly of being another Horace Greeley was a man now with his feet on the ground. Sometimes he did wonder what his life would have been like if he had struck out for the glittering metropolis in his younger days. Could he have climbed to the top rung in his profession? But no, facts were facts; he was a small-city publisher approaching middle age, and he was burdened with debts. He would be lucky if he came out of this money crisis with his modest reputation intact. The stir and bustle of New York were thrilling, but he could not feel comfortable in the city. He hated being away from Effie, and he hated begging from haughty bankers. "It is a very disagreeable business, this borrowing money," he wrote to Effie. "But I will get through with it some day, I hope."

The magnificent new *Times* plant kept inching skyward, before the fascinated eyes of Chattanoogans who already thought of it as a symbol of the city's progress, a landmark almost as distinctive as the city's own spectacular Lookout Mountain. And the *Times* itself kept on prospering; it truly was one of the South's most successful newspapers, earning about $25,000 a year. But impressive as this profit was, it could pay little more than the interest on his land boom loans.

To meet bills for granite, gold dome and the grand new press he had ordered, he went further into debt.

In the early 1890's, Ochs hardly knew a carefree hour. Every month he borrowed more, to pay the interest on money he had already borrowed. Only Effie knew how bad things were. His upright father would have shuddered at the peril of the financial swamp his son was sinking into. He would have warned him against borrowing another cent, but now his father was dead.

Adolph Ochs did spend anguished hours worrying if his pride in a gold dome had not put him on the path to ruin. The only possible end to his frenzied borrowing seemed bankruptcy. Sooner or later he would have to let the whole world know that he could not pay back these loans, that he was not many cuts above a common swindler. Once that happened, the courts would take over whatever property he still owned, and sell it to give back to trusting lenders at least a part of what was their due.

The prospect horrified him. To have his *Times*, his precious newspaper that he had built up from nothing, sold to the highest bidder would scar the rest of his life. On calmer reflection, Ochs realized that his future might not be quite that black, because he had a reputation as an honest man and as a newspaper publisher of talent. Quite possibly he would be allowed to keep the *Times*, and to run it himself under a court's supervision, till every creditor got some of his money. Paying back every penny would be out of the question. True the *Times* was prosperous, but it was no gold mine. Such a bankruptcy was comparatively painless, but it could leave his name tarnished forever.

Adolph spent hours of torture considering what to do. He would not stop work on the new building. He would not think of bankruptcy. He had to find more money somewhere. Very slowly an astonishing idea captured his mind.

Instead of casting about miserably, he would struggle out of this swamp like a man. Yes, he needed money but hadn't he proved to himself and to the world, that he knew how to make money respectably and honestly, by publishing a good newspaper? Well, if one good newspaper would not make enough to pay his debts, maybe two newspapers could.

Adolph Ochs set out to find another newspaper.

Another man in his shoes might have welcomed the comparative peace of bankruptcy. This man could not do so. Bedeviled by debt, he decided to take on even more debt, to gamble for even higher stakes. Instead of selling, he would buy another newspaper in another city and build it up till it had the same standing in its city that the *Times* had in Chattanooga—and the same prosperity, too. He began to scour the smaller cities of the South for a likely newspaper prospect.

At the same time, he swallowed one shred of pride about his gold dome. There was no other way except to take out a mortgage on the new building. Till now, he had borrowed without putting his building on the block; however, the kind of money he needed to tide him over the coming months could not possibly be raised any other way. He would have to take the risk. Sick at heart, he rode up to New York again to seek the best possible deal on this hateful mortgage. "It is the meanest business a man ever undertook," he wrote to Effie.

One trip was not enough to consummate the deal. He had to travel up repeatedly in the early months of 1892. He stayed in second-rate hotels to pinch pennies; he walked to save carfare. During these months, he had a new fear, too—and a new faint hope. After so long, Effie again was expecting a baby.

Only to her had he poured out all his problems. Her calm affection had steadied him through the hardest hours. Now the thought that her frail health might not stand another hard birth terrified him, and yet he could not suppress the hope that they might have a healthy child at last. To raise her spirits, he wired jubilantly when he finally closed a favorable mortgage deal in New York: "Put three quarts of champagne on ice. Ask Aunt Julia and the girls. Get up a swell dinner."

Home again, he relaxed after all this tension. Among her new books, Effie had a fancy leather *Album for Confessions*—where you filled in the answers to a lot of harmless questions, and then displayed it for the amusement of guests. In her clear, delicate handwriting, Effie had already finished her page:

> FAVORITE COLOR? The soft gray dove.
> FLOWER? Forget-me-not I dearly love.
> TREE? The sturdy oak so grand and tall.
> HOUR IN THE DAY? The dinner hour best of all.
> SEASON OF THE YEAR? The gentle spring time suits me well.
> NAMES MALE & FEMALE? Philip and Helen, if I must tell.
> POETS? Tennyson, Byron and Burns.
> PROSE AUTHOR? Dickens, Thackeray and Eliot by turns.
> CHARACTER IN ROMANCE? Maggie Tulliver, Tom and Philip and St. Isidore.
> CHARACTER IN HISTORY? Napoleon, Alexander and Sir Thomas More.
> WHAT BOOK NOT RELIGIOUS WOULD YOU PART WITH LAST? *The Mill on the Floss.*
> YOUR FAVORITE OCCUPATION? Just living, I think.

TRAITS OF CHARACTER YOU MOST
ADMIRE IN A MAN? Gentleness and a head
for drink.
TRAITS OF CHARACTER YOU MOST
ADMIRE IN A WOMAN? Capability of hold-
ing her peace.
TRAIT YOU MOST DETEST IN EACH?
Meanspirit, I detest in each.

Reading what his wife had written, Ochs got right into the spirit of the game. He took a pen and wrote rapidly:

FAVORITE COLOR? Blue

FLOWER? Maréchal Niel (a yellow, climbing
rose, then very popular)

TREE? Oak

HOUR IN THE DAY? Dinner hour

SEASON OF THE YEAR? Spring

NAMES MALE & FEMALE? John and Effie

POET? Pope

PROSE AUTHOR? Macauley

CHARACTER IN ROMANCE? Maggie Tulliver

CHARACTER IN HISTORY? Abraham Lincoln

WHAT BOOK NOT RELIGIOUS WOULD
YOU PART WITH LAST? *Webster's New
Unabridged Dictionary*

YOUR FAVORITE OCCUPATION? Journalism

TRAIT OF CHARACTER YOU MOST ADMIRE
IN A MAN? Reliability

TRAIT OF CHARACTER YOU MOST ADMIRE
IN A WOMAN? Sincerity

TRAIT YOU MOST DETEST IN EACH?
Dishonesty

Then Ochs added that if he were not himself, he would rather be President of the United States, and that his motto was " 'Tis patient toil ensures success."

From this mild confessing it was but a step to horseplay. One evening when his sisters were giving a proper, ladylike party that had involved much silver-polishing and doily-pressing in advance, he stopped on his way home to buy a sausage from a street cart. A few minutes later, he led donkey, cart and sausages right up the front steps of the Cedar Street house and offered to treat all the guests to a free snack. At first his sisters were aghast, then they giggled. They couldn't stay angry with Dolph.

A few months later, Ochs had to make another trip to New York, to sign more papers concerning the $75,000 mortgage he had secured. This time, he left Effie in Cincinnati to await the birth of their child. Considering her history, he had judged it wise to bring her where medical facilities were better than anything Chattanooga had to offer.

On September 18, 1892, Ochs received a joyful telegram. A daughter had been safely born and both mother and child were doing splendidly.

The evening train for Cincinnati had already left when Ochs got this wire at his hotel. He sent off a few giddy wires, then he told the chambermaid his great news, he told the bellboy, he told the desk clerk. Finally he found his way to the barroom, where he bought champagne for everyone and toasted his new daughter all through the night, hurrying to make the morning train.

Two days later, from Cincinnati, he wrote his mother in Chattanooga: "The child is a great big baby with much dark hair, eyes between blue and gray, a nose that seems inclined to be puggy. She has a double chin, the cutest of hands and nails. I bought the kid a handsome cloak and two pairs of infants shoes."

At last he had a child on whom to lavish his love. From his first sight of her, he doted on his daughter, named Iphigene after her mother.

With all his optimistic heart, he believed that her birth could be an omen of better times ahead for him. The $75,000 from the mortgage had settled his most pressing debts, making it possible for him to have a breathing spell. But he still owed too much—and he knew he would not be able to rest easy till he had freed his unfinished building from the threat the mortgage implied. And he had yet to find a suitable second newspaper.

He had quietly looked into a few possibilities, but held off making any decision, for he was absorbed in putting the last touches on his new plant in Chattanooga. Finally, on December 8, 1892, with a wintry sun shining down on its gold dome, his new home of the Chattanooga *Times* officially opened its doors, and during the day and evening 10,000 people pressed in to look around. The open house crowd jostled good-naturedly from basement to roof, staring in awe at the new monster press, the huge plate-glass windows in the counting-room, the newfangled elevators, the mysterious machines in the composing room that took the drudgery out of typesetting. Remembering his own early days, Ochs had bought one of the first linotype machines ever seen in the South.

This was a great day for Chattanooga, and the city did its best to show its appreciation. A surprise ceremony had been arranged, to thank Ochs on behalf of all his fellow citizens.

That evening Judge D. M. Key, who had been Postmaster General of the United States, presented a splendid gift to the publisher—a huge grandfather's clock that had been smuggled into the building earlier in the day. Below the face of the clock was a bronze plaque: "To Adolph S. Ochs—From the Citizens of Chattanooga."

Overcome with emotion, Ochs stepped forward to voice his gratitude:

> I shall endeavor not to go too fast or too slow but keep a regular, steady gait in the path of truth and fairness. Every evening before the paper goes to press I shall try to see that everything it contains will be timely and in season and I hope that the reader each morning will find it so. I believe this will be the case if I continue to have the encouragement, support and confidence of the people as I have in the past. I thank you deeply for this kind expression of your friendship and hope that I may continue in your estimation to be deserving of it. I cannot say anything more.

When the crowds thinned out, and after all the congratulatory messages had been read, Ochs faced his uncertain future again. He hated the hypocrisy he felt. Would he have heard all these fine tributes if the true state of his finances had been known? He was more determined than ever to pull himself out of this mess. But he couldn't seem to find a second newspaper that he really wanted. For most of the papers he had investigated, the publishers were asking far too much cash. His own fine reputation was a drawback in these negotiations, for people were not going to sell too cheaply to a man who could make a newspaper pay. In a few weeks he gloomily got on a train for New York again, to see about raising still another loan to tide him through the coming year.

It was to be a ghastly year, for him and many others. The panic of 1893, brought on by reckless railway financing and other unsound money practices, swept the nation in the early spring. Everywhere in the United States, business failed and unemployment soared. More than ever, bankers were loath to make loans, and Ochs had never scurried as desperately from bank to bank as he did in the ensuing months.

But in a way the general depression helped him. Other respected businessmen were floundering, too. It was no disgrace to be in a tight spot financially in '93. Close associates in Chattanooga had begun to suspect the true state of his affairs by now, but they helped cover up for him because of his unblemished record, and somehow he squeaked through.

At the height of the panic, Ochs kept his nerve. He borrowed from one man to pay another, and he boldly let it be known throughout the South that he was looking for a likely paper he could pick up cheaply. The long miserable months of this great business slump put him to the hardest test he had faced yet, and how he met this test proved the decisive fact of his life.

Instead of settling for the safest course, the easiest course, he chose the most challenging course.

Baby Iphigene was nearing her third birthday, and gray depression still gripped the land when Ochs made still another borrowing trip to New York in the spring of 1895. His hope of finding a second newspaper had almost faded, though he was still dickering listlessly for the Nashville *American*.

Money woes pressed him as badly as ever, and he was constantly plagued by thoughts of bankruptcy. Yet he *could* pay back every penny, he was positive of it, if he could only get his hands on another newspaper with a reasonable growth potential. In New York to beg cash again, he caught himself considering a far-fetched notion. Suppose he were to look for a New York newspaper?

This thought had been hiding in the back of his mind for a long time, ever since his barefoot boyhood. But now he was a grown man who prided himself on his good judgment. How, he asked himself, could a man teetering on the edge of bankruptcy even think of crashing the elite circle of New York publishers? New York City was the journalistic capital of the nation. The least impressive paper in town was bound to cost a small fortune; and to turn it into a good newspaper would take cash and push and brilliance far above the resources of a country upstart. Thus Adolph Ochs argued with himself, but he sat up late, studying every newspaper he could pick up in the lobby stand in his hotel.

The next morning, he went to call on the publisher of an entirely undistinguished journal called the New York *Mercury*.

This was a lowly sheet devoted to promoting the free silver movement, the controversial program of one branch of the Democratic party. In his Chattanooga *Times*, Ochs had opposed free silver. At the moment issues did not matter. The *Mercury* had a printing plant, it belonged to the United Press, which sent it general news—and its editorial policy could be changed.

Ochs did not march into the *Mercury* office completely unprepared. By now he had a small acquaintance among New York newspaperdom, and he had heard gossip that the paper might be up for sale. It didn't take long for him to have the gossip confirmed.

All that spring, and on into the summer, fall and winter, he negotiated with the *Mercury*'s owners in the hope of arriving at a mutually satisfactory deal. The paper's ownership wanted to sell, all right, but only on their own terms. They wanted $160,000—plus a promise that the paper would continue to back free silver.

A fever to buy in New York had infected Ochs, and it made him waver on the brink of weak compromise. He wrote Effie in Chattanooga:

> With the lights before me at present I am conscientiously opposed to the free coinage of silver, but I must admit also that this opinion is not the result of a thorough understanding of the question. I will admit that the science of the use of silver and gold as money is beyond my comprehension. You can appreciate the dilemma I am in. I shall do nothing until I return home.

This was wavering indeed from the man who had encouraged gray-bearded Colonel MacGowan to blast away at free silver on the Chattanooga *Times* editorial page. But Effie helped him to stand firm again. Despite her frail look, she had a keen mind and her husband relied on her judgment. After much consultation, he made up his own mind. He could not, in all conscience, agree to the *Mercury* terms. He could not run a newspaper if he had to dance to somebody else's tune, and the *Mercury*'s owners clearly expected to keep on calling the tune.

But Ochs was not prepared to give up quite yet. He sniffed around the *Mercury* plant, found that the paper was losing close to $2,000 a week. Surely the owners would have to relent soon; nobody could take a loss like this indefinitely. By late September, the proprietors were prepared to scale down their demands.

Ochs wrote Effie:

> At first they scorned the idea, but finally pro-
> posed to sell me half interest for $75,000, giving
> me control and a reasonable salary before division
> of the profits. I think they will eventually take
> $25,000 cash, provided another $25,000 goes into
> the treasury as working capital. Mr. Noble of the
> *Mercury* pretends to be greatly impressed with my
> ability to make a success.

All through the fall and winter, Ochs kept on dickering
with the *Mercury* people. At home in Chattanooga, he somehow found the time to squire Effie to musicales, and he ener-
getically superintended the arrangements for civic meetings
and dinner parties in his own rambling house. But still he
made repeated trips up to New York.

Effie and his mother had long since grown used to his
dashing about like a kindly whirlwind, and yet they worried
over him now. He was approaching middle age without
showing any signs of slowing down. When they urged him
to rest more, to take up a soothing hobby instead of squandering so much energy on work, he smilingly pooh-poohed
their suggestions. Work to him was like a tonic, he insisted.

So he kept hurrying back and forth to New York till
finally, in the early spring, his conditions were met by Mr.
Noble of the *Mercury*, and a deal seemed assured. Only
then did Ochs make a startling discovery. The *Mercury*'s
membership in the United Press would lapse if control of
the paper passed into new hands, so the paper would no
longer receive UP news for its columns. And in the com-
petitive climate then prevailing in New York journalism,
publishers of rival newspapers would surely veto a new
request for membership in the UP or Associated Press.

Ochs broke off the long negotiations at last, and late in March of 1896, shortly after his thirty-eighth birthday, dispiritedly caught a train back to Chattanooga.

Within a week, a telegram came from Harry Alloway, a financial news reporter whom Ochs had entertained once during a Chattanooga assignment and seen again during the *Mercury* dickering. The telegram made Ochs gasp. It said: "WOULD NEW YORK TIMES PROPOSITION BE ATTRACTIVE NOW? ANSWER CONFIDENTIAL."

Ochs reached for a pen and breathlessly wrote a reply asking for further details.

The following day, Ochs went to Chicago on a previously planned business trip. Lunching there with Herman H. Kohlsaat, publisher of the Chicago *Times-Herald*, who was an old friend from Associated Press meetings, Ochs confided he was quaking at the prospect of proposing himself as a possible purchaser of the renowned *New York Times*.

"I don't think I'm a big enough man for the job," Ochs said.

Kohlsaat smiled reassuringly. "Don't tell anybody," he said, "and they'll never find out."

From Chicago, Ochs boarded an eastbound train for New York City.

7

Unknown to the general public, *The New York Times* was sinking fast in 1896. Founded in 1851 by Henry J. Raymond, who had helped Horace Greeley put out his first *Tribune* ten years earlier, the *Times* quickly leaped to newspaper eminence under the partnership of Raymond and George Jones, a banker-turned-editor. This team made the *Times* a solid, conservative daily, highly regarded by the city's business community and unquestionably one of New York's journalistic ornaments, along with Greeley's *Tribune*, James Gordon Bennett's *Herald* and later Charles A. Dana's *Sun*. After Raymond's death in 1869, Jones ran the *Times* by himself, bringing it added luster in the eyes of respectable citizens by waging newspaper war on the corrupt Tammany Hall political machine and unseating Tammany's notorious Boss Tweed. But when Jones died in 1891, the paper had already begun to lose readers by antagonizing its staunch Republican following, and Jones's heirs proceeded to lose even more by printing a weak, undistinguished paper.

Not really interested in running a newspaper, they soon tried to sell it—for more than $1,000,000. This figure reflected the prestige the *Times*'s name had won, not its true value at the time; they found no takers.

To the ordinary New Yorker, the *Times* still looked solid, if unreadable, stacked high on the city's newsstands. But insiders sensed a creeping decay. As a desperate step, a group of *Times* employees bought out the Jones heirs in 1893—for less than $1,000,000. Whatever the actual sum, they got no bargain, because the *Times* plant had been allowed to run down miserably, and the new management had not a penny of working capital or a jot of big-time business experience. Charles R. Miller, editor of the paper and now its boss, was a thoughtful writer nurtured on a New Hampshire farm. But unlike that other New Hampshire farm boy, Horace Greeley, he did not have the magic touch it took to run a successful New York daily on his own. The *Times,* by 1896, seemed headed for an early death.

This was the newspaper Adolph Ochs yearned to own. It fit his plans exactly: it had a great name and a tremendous growth potential, and it *might* be for sale. How shaky the paper actually was he did not yet know. For now, the mere thought of trying for such a prize made his pulse race. What a chance this was! Could a boy's dream really come true?

But Ochs was by now a man of some business sophistication, and he knew that to buy the *Times* he would have to break into a new league financially as well as journalistically—the big league of Wall Street tycoons like J. P. Morgan and August Belmont. Nobody could swing the purchase of a property like *The New York Times* on his own; it was a major corporation with powerful stockholders who had put their money into its stocks and bonds. While the group of employees headed by Miller were in charge of the paper's day-to-day operations, the real power rested with the hardheaded stockholders behind the scenes. Ochs knew he would have to win good will and cash in the highest places if he were to succeed.

He wrote from New York on March 27, 1896:

> My darling Wife and Baby,
>
> I doubt if there are many men in these United States who are as subject to the caprices of circumstances as I am. Here I am in New York ready to negotiate for the leading and most influential newspaper in America.
>
> Now for the supreme gall of a country newspaperman burdened with debt. Alloway thinks I am the man—the ideal man—for the *Times*. . . .

This Alloway, who had been reporting financial news for the *Times* since 1879, not only pushed Ochs to think of buying the paper, but he also spread the word where it would count most that Ochs could save the *Times*.

He assured Charles R. Flint, the largest holder of *Times* stock, that Ochs had already worked the same kind of miracle in Chattanooga where he had built the Chattanooga *Times* from a $250 shoestring. Then Alloway let Ochs know that Flint was a close personal friend of President Grover Cleveland, and suggested that a word of recommendation from the President could not fail to help.

Ochs remembered President Cleveland. Their conversation in Chattanooga on the day rain had reddened the young publisher's borrowed overcoat led him to hope the President would put in a good word for him. To Effie he wrote:

> Alloway took dinner with me tonight. He is a schemer from 'way back yonder, but he is very

much in earnest. He sincerely believes that I can get the *Times*. Tonight I am going to write to Grover Cleveland to grant me an interview for Sunday, and I am going to ask a letter from him to Flint. How's that for cheek?

Ochs at this point had no clear idea of how he could go about getting control of the *Times*. In theory, it was still worth about $1,000,000; shares of stock in that amount were outstanding. No matter if this stock would not bring much on the open market, it still did have substantial value because of the newspaper's great name. Alloway tried to convince Ochs that Flint's $550,000 in stock could be bought for one-fourth of its face value, and that other, smaller stockholders, including Morgan and Belmont, who each owned $25,000 worth, would then fall into line. Ochs let himself be convinced; he was not fazed by the fact that one-fourth of $1,000,000 was still $250,000. And how could a debt-ridden country newspaperman raise that kind of money?

Bubbling, heedless of sober common sense, Ochs dashed off letters to President Cleveland and to about fifty other influential men in many walks of life—publishers, editors, railroad men, congressmen, ministers.

He told them:

> I am negotiating for a controlling interest in *The New York Times*, and have fair prospects of success. I write to respectfully ask that you address by return mail a letter to Mr. Spencer Trask, chairman of the New York Times Publishing Company, giving your opinion on my qualifications as a newspaper publisher, general personal character, and my views on public questions, judged by the course of the Chattanooga *Times*.

In other words, say what you can of me as an honest, industrious and capable newspaper publisher. I wish to assure you that the enterprise I contemplate is not too large for me. I am able to handle it financially and otherwise.

This brash letter brought results. Within thirty-six hours, President Cleveland wrote back:

In your management of the Chattanooga *Times* you have demonstrated such a faithful adherence to Democratic principles, and have so bravely supported the ideas and policies which tend to the safety of our country as well as our party, that I should be glad to see you in a larger sphere of usefulness. If your plans are carried out, and if through them you are transferred to metropolitan journalism, I wish you the greatest measure of success possible.

And every other man on Ochs's list wrote a similar letter. An old friend, Leopold Wallach, a New York lawyer, excitedly offered his help. He arranged for Ochs to meet several *Times* stockholders he knew, and he offered legal advice. With a rush, the stage was being set for serious Wall Street talk on the possibilities of selling control of *The New York Times* to penniless Adolph Ochs from Chattanooga.

Dashing off wires to MacGowan every day suggesting Chattanooga *Times* editorials, Ochs kept his feet close to the ground, although his head seemed in the clouds. But his letters home sounded so outlandish that his wife and mother worried. They even thought he might be not quite well, and sent his Uncle George up to see him. He had a hard time convincing Uncle George that he was better than he'd ever been and sent him back home.

There was still one man he had to win over to his cause. This was Charles R. Miller, the editor-in-chief of the *Times*, whose estimate of a buyer's newspaper talent would surely have a profound influence on any financier's decision.

Alloway arranged for Ochs to call on Miller at the Millers' West Fifty-fifth Street home one evening after dinner. Miller was so certain that nothing would come of this meeting that he had promised to take his wife and children to the theatre after spending only a polite few minutes with the Chattanooga stranger. He had heard too many silly plans for saving the *Times* already. What could this unknown southerner have to offer?

After waiting only a token ten minutes, Mrs. Miller knocked on the door of the study where her husband was sitting with Ochs. "We'll miss the opening, dear," she called.

Miller opened the door. He smiled reassuringly at his wife. "You go along ahead of me with the children," he said. "I'll join you later." But he did not. He sat listening to Ochs in his own study through the first act and the second act and the third act, and he was still sitting with him when his family came home after the final curtain. Not till after one o'clock in the morning did the door of his study open and the hypnotic stranger from Chattanooga depart.

What did Ochs tell Miller that night? Neither man ever said, but Ochs must have summoned up a masterfully eloquent argument about how he could put *The New York Times* back on its feet. At a moment of supreme importance, Ochs could give a magnificent sales talk; and from then on Miller was staunchly in his corner as Ochs fought to clear away financial obstacles and assume control of the great, ailing daily.

Miller gave Ochs a glowing build-up to Flint and to financier Spencer Trask, chairman of the stockholders' board of directors. They agreed to see Ochs.

"I know I can manage the *Times* as a decent, dignified and independent newspaper and still wipe out the deficit," Ochs told them firmly. "I could change your hundred-thousand-dollar-a-year loss into at least a forty-thousand-dollar-a-year surplus."

This, and a column of figures to show the financial ways and means he had in mind, bowled the two men over. They conferred alone for a few minutes, then offered Ochs a job— the job of managing the *Times* for them at a fixed but handsome salary.

"We're prepared to pay you fifty thousand dollars a year," Trask told him.

Ochs bluntly turned the offer down.

"I simply will not take the job for merely a fixed salary, not even if you offer me a hundred and fifty thousand a year," he said. "I am not looking for employment. Unless you offer me eventual control of the property— based, of course, on my making good—there is no sense in keeping on with these negotiations. I am merely trying to say, Mr. Trask, that if I can bring about the results I have outlined, I am entitled to something more than a fixed salary."

He was staggered at his own effrontery, but he had said exactly what he believed. Tensely he waited a week for Trask and Flint to consult their fellow stockholders, and while he waited Alloway brought him an alarming rumor.

He reported that a group of smaller stockholders had decided the day of the conservative newspaper had passed.

The big newspaper excitement in New York now was the vicious fight between Joseph Pulitzer's *World* and William Randolph Hearst's *Journal*, both lively, sensational papers. These stockholders felt only a sensational sheet could survive, and they aimed to combine the *Times* with another dying paper, the undistinguished *Recorder*, and then print a *Times-Recorder* as bold and sensational as anything Pulitzer or Hearst could offer.

Ochs was appalled by this plan. No newspaper in New York, even the respected *Times*, fully met his own high standards; even the *Times* had been known to stoop to name-calling and airing private grievances in print. But the *Times* approached impartiality more often than most other newspapers, and the thought that it, too, might start sinking made him press Miller for prompt action. Conservative editor Miller was just as appalled as Ochs at the idea of turning the *Times* into a gaudy scandal sheet. To block this, he took a drastic step and had the *Times* declared bankrupt, so that the stockholders no longer could dispose of it themselves. A court-appointed receiver now would have the decisive say. If Miller's maneuver was bold, it was justified, for with $300,000 in back bills and a new loss of about $2,500 every week the *Times* was entitled to take refuge in bankruptcy.

The receiver appointed to search out the best possible solution of this financial mess, a lawyer named Alfred Ely, approached Adolph Ochs with suspicion. None of the New York newspapermen Ely had talked to would give the *Times* a ghost of a chance to compete successfully with the city's established papers like the *Sun, Herald* and *Tribune*, let alone against the battling *World* and *Journal.* Ochs insisted, though, that he could do it.

By now he had worked out an intricate financial plan that conceivably could achieve his own ends, settle the *Times*'s debts and enrich its stockholders, too. This called for the formation of a new company that would issue 10,000 new shares of stock, worth $100 apiece. Holders of old *Times* stock would exchange five old shares for one new one. Then, in addition, the new company would float a big bond issue. Three hundred thousand dollars in bonds would be given to the business concerns and individuals who were owed money by the *Times*. If the paper should prosper, in time the creditors would be paid back every penny when they turned in their bonds, and meanwhile they would be receiving five percent interest on their money every year. On top of this, another $400,000 in bonds would be sold to raise cash for *Times* operating expenses.

Who in his right mind would buy any of these latter bonds, at $1,000 apiece? What investor would even consider putting good money into such a risky business? But Adolph Ochs said he could sell the bonds and Alfred Ely said: "Go ahead and try."

A dynamo working at an incredible pace, Ochs set out to sell the bonds. As a lure, he offered fifteen free shares of stock to every bond-buyer—then he clinched his own eventual control of the *Times* by scraping up $75,000 to buy bonds in his own name, thus automatically acquiring 1,125 shares of stock; with an additional 3,876 shares of stock Trask agreed to hold in a bank vault for him till he could make the paper pay its expenses for three consecutive years, he would eventually hold a total of 5,001 shares of the 10,000 outstanding.

How he got hold of $75,000 is impossible to say. But at this point in his life, Ochs had the persuasive powers of a master hypnotist. Up and down Wall Street, he talked tough-minded money kings into lending him their money, into buying bond certificates that would be worthless scraps unless he performed the miracle of making *The New York Times* prosper again.

Ochs put every ounce of his strength into this masterly performance. For more than three months, he went at a rate that would have killed stronger men. In a letter to Effie one evening, he scribbled a list of the appointments he had kept during the day:

> At Flint's office at 10 o'clock. Wallach's office, 10:20. Belmont's 11. Hanover Bank, 12. Wallach's, 12:30. Wilson & Wallace, 12:45. Western Union, 1:20. Lunch, 1:45. Western Union, 2. Hartley's, 2:30. Hanover Bank, 3. Wallach's, 3:20. Hartley's, 4. Glens Falls Paper, 4:15. New York *Sun*, 4:45. Van Doren's, 5. N.Y. *Post* Job Printing, 5:15. Julian F. Davis, 5:20. Charles R. Flint, 5:35.

Some days he did not allow himself even fifteen minutes for lunch. Every quarter hour had to count. On June 16th, he wrote to Effie: "It took me just fifteen minutes this morning to get J. P. Morgan's signature on the agreement to exchange his old stock for new. The United Press signed." And nine other creditors signed agreements the same day to accept *Times* bonds for outstanding debts. He charmed one stockholder after another. He wrote Effie about financier Jacob Schiff.

> It is a great story. Mr. Schiff has $25,000 in old *Times* stock that cost him $25,000 cash, but he told

me to come again tomorrow and he would give me
the certificate and I could do with it as I pleased.
He said he wanted no interest, and could give no
encouragement to a newspaper with Democratic
leanings. He said he had been a Mugwump, but
henceforth he would be Republican. He made me
a present of the stock. Of course, he thinks it has
no value but it will get $5,000 of new stock, and I
hope to make that worth par in less than three
years.

Through the hot, dusty weeks of a New York summer,
Ochs never stopped. So keyed up that he could not rest even
on weekends, he bought himself a bicycle outfit for five dollars, hired a bicycle in Central Park and rode miles through
the steaming city. One afternoon, he rode from the park in
Manhattan all the way down to the Brooklyn Bridge, then
across Brooklyn to the beach at Coney Island. That night he
slept soundly.

Ochs got every signature he needed. Gradually, seeing
his prize in reach, he slowed down a little, but a court had to
approve the sale of the bankrupt *Times*. Finally, August 13
was fixed for the court session that would consider his offer,
and as the day approached, frightening rumors erupted. He
wrote to Effie that he had heard that "some Monte Cristo," a
mysterious millionaire, was set to put in a competing bid for
the paper. "Also Arkell of *Judge* Magazine is said to be itch-
ing for it. There is a rich man from Troy said to be quietly in
the field. The *Recorder* consolidation group is supposed to
have something up its sleeve. There's another rumor about
some rich Chicago banker—a very rich man named
Torrence, with money to burn. They say he wants to buy the
Times to out-Hearst Hearst. The air is full of such stories."

Then, with quiet confidence, Ochs added:

"I believe I am master of the situation. I don't believe anyone will compete after they learn my true strength. To defeat me at the sale they will have to have more money than sense. *I will win*; put that down."

And he did win. Not another bidder turned up at the court. "My Darling Wife and Baby," Ochs wrote five evenings later, a few hours after he had formally taken over the publisher's office in the Park Row building of *The New York Times*:

> The first *New York Times* letter sheet I use carries my love to those who are dearer to me than the great prize I have won. I was formally installed at 3:30 P.M. today, and an army of men stands ready to carry out my wishes. I have succeeded way beyond my fondest hopes, and with God's help I will maintain the position with credit. I am a lucky fellow . . . I will move from the Madison Avenue Hotel to the Astor House tomorrow. I will reside there till you come. Address your mail care of *The New York Times*.

8

Effie read this letter aloud to the assembled Ochs family, and when her gentle voice had finished there was a silence in the comfortable parlor on Cedar Street in Chattanooga. Sadness hung in the air as the unspoken truth burst on them. Now this would no longer be Dolph's home. His place, and Effie's, from now on would be far off in New York City. All other considerations of worldly success vanished at the wrenching thought that the close family ties were inevitably to be severed now. Then Mama Ochs, plump and sturdy, reached for the letter she herself had just received.

She read:

> It is a matter of the greatest pride to me that I have enabled my mother to say that she is the mother of the publisher of *The New York Times*. I am here safely in the position which puts me in the front rank of the newspaper men of the world; a position which I one time, not long ago, thought as impossible for me as the throne of Great Britain. If I have succeeded far beyond what is ordinarily

man's lot, I owe much to the influence of a mother who is the noblest and purest of mortal beings. God bless her and preserve her for many years to see her son prove himself worthy of the good fortune which has befallen him.

What would be would be. There was no arguing with it. A babble of voices rose in the parlor as Dolph's brothers and sisters all started to discuss the suddenly different future.

Brother George, now a respected editor and no longer a gun-toting dandy, would undoubtedly be in charge of the Chattanooga *Times*. With Milton, he had been running the paper for the last three months, and Dolph's wires from New York had hardly been necessary. George would be general manager now, aided by Milton and by Ada's husband, Henry C. Adler.

The family would keep the Cedar Street house, of course. Mama was too set in her ways to think of moving—and moving North was completely out of the question, for she was a pillar in the Daughters of the Confederacy and despite the tinge of Bavaria in her speech, a true lady of the old South. As always, she would be surrounded by children and grandchildren, good-humoredly clucking over them all—all but Dolph and Effie and Iphigene, still called Baby. Their home would be far away now, but Effie assured them they would come often on visits and this would still be their real home. A flurry of happy-sad wires and letters descended on Adolph Ochs in New York City.

Amid his thousand chores, he wrote back his approval of their ideas. He sent detailed suggestions to George and Milton and Harry, but he assured them that running the Chattanooga paper would be their responsibility from now on. He wired a plea to Effie to come up to the beach at Atlantic City in New

Jersey as soon as possible with Baby, so that he could spend weekends with them till New York cooled off and they could move into a house there.

"Kiss my little darling for me," he wrote, "and tell her her Papa would like very much to see her and carry her around on his shoulders and on his back; that he fears that if he prolongs his absence much longer she will be too large for him to carry around."

Ochs may have feared a little that his almost-four-year-old daughter would forget him, but he had no qualms about the fearful business responsibility he had assumed. Although in the eyes of most knowing journalists the newspaper he had taken over was a wreck, he saw the situation quite differently with his own clear, confident blue eyes. Now that he had control of *The New York Times*, he felt he had nothing to worry about. That he had to make a dying paper pay its way for three consecutive years before he would truly have control seemed to him a mere detail; he had not a doubt in the world that he would succeed.

On his first full day in charge of *The New York Times*, Ochs quietly walked into the cubbyhole office of the circulation manager, the man responsible for getting the paper onto the city's newsstands. Without a word, the circulation man locked the door of his little office behind them, then with a second key opened his battered rolltop desk, from which he withdrew a sheaf of penciled figures.

While Ochs had suspected the worst, nevertheless the figures shocked him. Of 19,000 papers printed daily and delivered by horse-drawn wagons to stands all over the city, at least 10,000 copies were being returned unsold every evening. The circulation of the great *New York Times* was down to a melancholy 9,000 a day.

"Circulation will soon be increased," Ochs said gently.

"Increased?" the circulation man said. "Increased? Mr. Ochs, if you could keep it from going down any further, you would be a wonder man."

In 1896, close to 3,000,000 people lived in New York City and the population kept increasing every month as thousands of immigrants poured off ships to make new homes there. Not every man, woman and child counted by the census-taker, or even every family, was a potential newspaper buyer, but the city had a huge newspaper-reading public. In 1896, the circulation figures for New York dailies stood as follows:

Evening World, 400,000; *Morning Journal*, 300,000; *Morning World*, 200,000; *News*, 145,000; *Herald*, 140,000; *Evening Journal*, 130,000; *Morning Sun*, 70,000; *Evening Sun*, 60,000; *Post*, 19,000; *Press*, 18,000; *Tribune*, 16,000; *Advertiser*, 12,000; *Times*, 9,000; *Mail and Express*, 3,000; and *Commercial Advertiser*, 2,500.

Already the *Dispatch* and the *Recorder* had gone out of business, and several other papers were on their way to death or merger. But the morning and evening editions of Joseph Pulitzer's *World* were selling a daily total of 600,000 copies, and the two editions of Hearst's *Journal* a total of 430,000. These young papers, with their bold, black headlines, their flashy human interest stories, their comic strips, clearly dominated the market and were changing the face of journalism in the city. Hearst and Pulitzer, in their frantic rivalry, had both wooed the creator of a popular comic strip called "The Yellow Kid," and because the yellow-inked comic had appeared in the *World* and then the *Journal*, these were commonly called "the yellow papers," and their slam-bang style of presenting the news, "yellow journalism."

Both Hearst and Pulitzer knew exactly what they were doing. Hearst was a handsome young man from San Francisco with a seemingly bottomless treasure of his father's mining money to spend on the toy he craved most— a successful New York City newspaper. Pulitzer was a nervous, brilliant immigrant who had already made a spectacular success of the St. Louis *Post-Dispatch*. Despite the difference in backgrounds and temperament, both had picked the same formula for making their newspapers appeal to the widest possible number of readers; and to beat each other at the same game, they were putting up a fight with bank books and sensational journalism.

Even if Ochs had had the cash to compete with them, he would not have tried. He wanted to attract readers, too, but readers who would appreciate hard facts about a city election more than juicy scandal about an aging actress.

Ochs felt sure he could compete successfully among New York's old-line papers that had not given in to sensationalism. Each had a distinctive personality—the *Herald*'s mildly eccentric, the *Sun*'s literary, the *Tribune*'s solid Republican. Not one of these was doing the newspaper job that Ochs thought could and should be done in New York City, the job of providing all the plain, unvarnished news a competent staff could gather.

He planned to put out exactly that sort of newspaper he had dreamed about when he was still a printer's devil in Knoxville. Sitting down at his desk on Park Row to write his statement of aims as the new publisher of *The New York Times*, he penned these words:

To undertake the management of *The New York Times*, with its great history for right-doing, and to attempt to keep bright the lustre which Henry J. Raymond and George Jones have given it, is an extraordinary task. But if a sincere desire to conduct a high-standard newspaper, clean, dignified and trustworthy, requires honesty, watchfulness, earnestness, industry and practical knowledge, applied with common sense, I entertain the hope that I can succeed in maintaining the high estimate that thoughtful, pure-minded people have ever had of *The New York Times*.

It will be my earnest aim that *The New York Times* give the news, all the news, in concise and attractive form, in language that is parliamentary in good society, and give it as early, if not earlier, than it can be learned through any other reliable medium; to give the news impartially, without fear or favor, regardless of any party, sect or interest involved; to make the columns of *The New York Times* a forum for the consideration of all questions of public importance, and to that end to invite intelligent discussion from all shades of opinion.

There will be no radical changes in the personnel of the present efficient staff. Mr. Charles R. Miller, who has so ably for many years presided over the editorial paper, will continue to be the editor; nor will there be a departure from the general tone and character and policies pursued with relation to public questions that have distinguished *The New York Times* as a nonpartisan newspaper—unless it be, if possible, to intensify its devotion to the cause of sound money and tariff reform, opposition to wastefulness and speculation in administering the public affairs and in its advocacy of the lowest tax consistent with good government, and no more government than is absolutely necessary to protect society, maintain individual vested rights and secure the free exercise of a sound conscience.

Making his debut on the New York stage, Ochs found at once that a bright spotlight was shining on him. This statement was reprinted in newspapers throughout the country, and the sharp clarity of one phrase—"to give the news impartially, without fear or favor, regardless of any party, sect or interest involved"—won wide comment. In seventeen words, Ochs had summed up his own philosophy, and he had also stated a superb credo for free newspapermen everywhere.

But for every conscientious reader who plowed through his every word and applauded heartily, there were dozens left dubious. Who was this little man who had mysteriously seized control of a famous newspaper? Wasn't he just a puppet, put in power by J. P. Morgan or some other hidden potentate? Not a bit flurried by all the unfriendly rumors blowing round his head, Ochs set to work running the *Times*.

Early and late, he walked through his dusty domain, getting to know his staff, absorbing every detail of the paper's operation. From the very first, he was the kind of boss who gently suggested instead of issuing orders, who kept the door of his office open and genially greeted any employee appearing at the threshold, instead of barricading himself behind a bank of secretaries.

At thirty-eight, his thick black hair was starting to gray, he was tending toward the portly side and his manner in public was grave. The high, stiff collars he wore gave him a formal air. Added to this, he had the habit of addressing every man who worked for him, from printer to editor, as "Mr.," consequently he was "Mr. Ochs" to everybody. But proper Victorian gentleman though he was, he also had a wonderfully human smile that shone through pompous words and starchy manners. People liked him, trusted him, loved him.

In his first weeks, Ochs moved gingerly for he did not want to step on anyone's toes, if he could avoid it. Only for incompetence proved to his own satisfaction would he fire a man.

His first innovations were minor: he cut out the romantic fiction that had been cluttering a few *Times* columns a day; he threw away cases of tiny type so the paper would be easier to read; he bought better ink and paper. One night he paid a visit to the composing room and talked to his printers. "I'm a printer, as you are," he told them. "I've done my turn at the case with handset type. I want to make the *Times* the best example of the printing art in the whole newspaper field, and I know that with your help I can do it."

Then he added: "I'll keep my office door open to any *Times* man, at any time. That goes for the chief editor and it goes for the printers and the boy who sweeps the composing room floor." After shaking hands all around, the new boss departed, leaving the most eager printing crew any publisher could want. In the next issue of their union newspaper, the printers gave him their highest praise: "He is a practical printer who worked up from office boy."

Only nine days after Ochs took over in Park Row, a newspaper trade magazine called the *Newspapermaker* observed:

> A glance at *The New York Times* since it has been in the hands of Adolph S. Ochs is like a gleam of sunlight on a cloudy day. The professional sees at once the handiwork of a fellow artist. With the reputation of printing on the worst presses in the city, *The New York Times* now appears a typographical beauty.

The former office boy slowly began to make significant news changes, too. For example, he encouraged his new financial editor, Harry Alloway, to expand the paper's business and financial section until, within a few months, it became the most complete record of the city's commercial life that any newspaper had ever published. Other editors scoffed at first that all these columns of trade and market news made the *Times* deadly dull, but Ochs knew what he was about. Businessmen by the hundreds began buying the *Times* for its business news, and circulation inched back up toward the 15,000 mark.

Equally important, financial advertising doubled, tripled, then quadrupled. The *Times* was still far from paying its way, but every week its losses were lower. By the time other editors had caught on, Ochs had put the *Times* far into the lead in the business league and they could not overtake him there.

Then, spurred on by Effie, Ochs started to print a Saturday book review supplement. This was instantly popular, and brought in book ads, too. Soon the separate section was shifted to the Sunday paper, where it became the book trade's choice showplace for advertising, and the informed reader's indispensable guide to new books.

Another early Ochs innovation was a Sunday magazine section. Other papers had Sunday magazines, too, but theirs printed florid drawings illustrating poor fiction, or hokum feature stories often quite as fictional as the outright fiction. Ochs's magazine, illustrated with the best halftones money could buy then, contained well-written articles timed to point up current news: a history of the opera in New York when the opera season was about to start, a feature on famous horses when the horse show came to town, a piece about Queen Victoria as her birthday approached.

Schoolteachers and ministers began to praise the *Times* and circulation kept inching up. One day in September, the previously dour circulation manager sent a memo to Ochs reporting: "Newsboy on Brooklyn side of the bridge told me this morning that he very nearly had a fit one day this week. He sold all his *Times,* something he'd never done before, and not only that one day, but every day since." Owners of large Manhattan department stores, who had long since stopped advertising in the *Times*, began to invite Ochs to dinner, to sound him out about contracts for advertising space.

"I have an endless task ahead of me," Ochs wrote to Effie in Atlantic City, "but I find it pleasant, even in this steaming climate."

Late in September, he was still looking for a New York house for his family, still writing Effie every night as she waited at the Jersey shore. Cutting his ties with Chattanooga had been hard for Ochs; in fact, he never really did it altogether. Though he gave over the direction of the Chattanooga *Times* to his brothers, he could not give up thinking of Chattanooga as his home. Finally he rented a comfortable apartment in a small brick house on East Thirty-ninth Street, near Lexington Avenue, where Effie and Baby joined him. However, he would never stop thinking of himself as a Chattanoogan, and even after his mother's death he kept in close touch with family and friends there.

But New York absorbed the greatest part of his prodigious energy. Besides studying every facet of the *Times*, Ochs studied the whole great city his first fall there. How could he make a mark in the sprawling metropolis if he didn't know New York the way he had known Chattanooga? In October, he made a shrewd guess about New Yorkers' psychology. They would talk about a newspaper with a catchy slogan, he decided, and he thought up this slogan for the *Times*: "All the News That's Fit to Print." He hired a billboard at Twenty-third Street and Broadway, then a busy, fashionable intersection, and a lighted electric sign flashed his slogan to every passerby.

Ochs was amazed at the talk and letters provoked by his new slogan, which he also printed below the *Times* masthead on the editorial page. These seven words aroused quite a furor, because some people thought they sounded priggish; others that they seemed to be condoning censorship.

Along with Ochs's emphasis on pure language, the slogan may seem slightly absurd today, but in the 1890's gutter language was beginning to appear in other newspapers, to the horror of many right-thinking citizens like Ochs. It seemed necessary to campaign for purity in print. But Ochs rejected any thought that he might favor censorship of legitimate news.

"Then what's not fit to print?" he was asked.

"What is not true," he answered.

Still controversy about the slogan raged, and Ochs cheerfully took advantage of the public interest. He announced a contest for a new slogan, and offered a prize of $100, then every day for weeks he printed more than a column of entries. From as far away as San Francisco, other newspapers discussed the issue of *The New York Times* slogan and the San Francisco *Argonaut* wrote: "Realizing that the sewer and morgue fields were fully occupied by the *World* and the *Journal*, Ochs determined to issue a clean paper for a change. Very much to the surprise of himself and New York, he is making a success of it." It would have been impossible for the *Times* to buy any better advertising.

Then after a month of considering such contest entries as "Free From Filth, Full of News" and "News for the Million, Scandal for None," a panel of non-*Times* judges awarded the contest prize to D. M. Redfield of New Haven, Connecticut. His entry? "All the World News, but not a School for Scandal."

One hundred dollars the poorer, but infinitely richer in prestige, Adolph Ochs decided to keep his own "All the News That's Fit to Print," after all. In fact, he put it outside on the front page of *The New York Times* in a box opposite the box with the day's weather forecast, where it still appears today.

Flushed with this small triumph, Ochs did not make the mistake of assuming his troubles were over. The figures in the circulation manager's roll-top desk were looking better— but not good enough. Not good enough if the *Times* auditor was to stop writing reports in red ink.

Right at this time, when another man might be getting discouraged because a few months of sharpening and tightening had failed to take the *Times* out of the red, temptation was waved in front of Ochs's eyes. Early in the autumn, a big chunk of advertising was offered to him by the leaders of Tammany Hall.

According to law, the city had to advertise for bids before any contract for public construction could be authorized— and for years Tammany had been using this advertising as a polite handout to friendly publishers. In 1896, it proposed to divide about $200,000 in city money among six newspapers, each paper to receive about $30,000 for printing identical, unreadable ads, set in tiny print. The *Times* desperately needed $30,000, but Ochs stopped to consider.

He ordered his City Hall man to look into the law on the subject and found that advertising for bids was legal if it appeared in only one newspaper of general circulation.

So, even though he was starving for cash, Adolph Ochs printed a story denouncing Tammany for squandering city funds by duplicating the ads in five other papers. He turned down the *Times*'s share of this polite graft, causing Tammany and some other publishers to issue threats, but the respect Ochs gained from his staff and among the general public was worth it. If the *Times* was in the red, he would bring it out of the red honorably, of that he was still positive.

9

The presidential campaign of 1896 was a flamboyant affair. Spellbinder William Jennings Bryan with his fiery free-silver preaching won the Democratic nomination; his opponent was solid Republican Ohioan William McKinley. Bands blared across the nation and great, sizzling torches lit gaudy parades as ardent free-silverites and sound-money men vied for votes. Making his first appearance on the national political scene—for the publisher of a New York daily inevitably carries substantial political weight—Adolph Ochs found himself in something of a quandary.

By upbringing and conviction, Ochs was a Democrat but a conservative Democrat. He distrusted the radicals and reformers who tended to sweep to prominence in his party; in fact, he thought too many crackpots cropped up in Democratic colors, and that it was important for the political health of the nation for a goodly number of sober, right-thinking citizens to fight this crackpot influence from within the party instead of gravitating to the predictably conservative Republicans.

As publisher of *The New York Times*, Ochs had pledged his newspaper to the cause of sound money. Then wasn't he honor-bound to support McKinley, the soundest of sound-money men? Ochs did not think so. Every newspaper must have a personality, and he wanted his to have a conservative but Democratic editorial page. What he did was to throw his support to a splinter faction of sound-money Democrats.

With a boyish fervor, he leaped into the fight. Heading a delegation of fifty of his staff, all carrying silk banners that said "*The New York Times*," he strutted up Broadway one rainy October afternoon in a glorious sound-money parade—and Miller wrote ringing editorials backing a hopeless slate of gold Democrats. Whether money should be coined on the basis of the nation's gold supply alone, or whether gold and silver both should be used, was the main issue in the election; and as McKinley stood squarely for the first policy and Bryan for the second, this splinter ticket of anti-Bryan Democrats had not a chance of election.

In theory, Ochs and other Democrats who could not stomach free silver were registering a conscientious protest by refusing to vote for Bryan. In practice, they were merely helping McKinley's cause. This cold reality was appreciated by people who had had their doubts about Ochs from the day he took over the *Times*. "What better proof do you want that the man has sold out to Wall Street?" they asked. "But what do you expect of a Morgan puppet?"

Ochs carried on, unperturbed. Although his own financial situation was still murky, to put it mildly, and although he had done more tricks with money than most men, he had a deep and sincere belief that a sound money system—meaning, to him, a gold-based system—was essential for the fiscal well-being of the United States. He distrusted and disliked William Jennings Bryan. He thought Bryan unfit for the Presidency.

As much a realist as any of his detractors, Ochs understood that he was helping McKinley toward election. As Election Day approached, he plainly admitted to Effie that he passionately hoped for the Ohioan's victory.

On Election Night, once the polls were closed, carnival spirit erupted. The only way to find out how the vote was going was to join the crowd outside one of the newspaper offices, where big, crayoned bulletins were posted on a board every few minutes. Every newspaper had its bulletin board, where the latest telegraph news was posted every day of the year, but traditionally on Election Night great mobs assembled for word of the outcome and newspapers competed with each other to provide quick, dramatic outdoor reports.

This year, Hearst's *Journal* had built a great bandstand outside its plant and hired a brass band to toot away in between the posting of election returns. A chalk artist was on hand, too, to amuse the waiting crowd.

Not to be outdone, Pulitzer had built a giant, eighty-foot screen outside his *World*, onto which figures were flashed from a sort of slide machine.

Ochs had no money for such lavish shows. All he could manage were some special bulletin boards set in the windows of his Park Row building. Uptown at Twenty-third Street, beneath his "All the News That's Fit to Print" sign, he had a twenty-foot screen for flashing slides. Ochs left the *Times* building near City Hall about ten o'clock in the evening—

when the trend toward a McKinley victory already was becoming clear—and it took a couple of helmeted police-men to get him through the crowd. More than 50,000 people had come down to City Hall Park to watch his boards and Pulitzer's giant screen around the corner. But up at Twenty-third Street, the crowd was even larger. "Not bad!" he bragged to Effie, when he got home late that night. In this department, he aimed to compete with Pulitzer. He told her:

"I couldn't help thinking as I watched our display how interested I was in the outcome of the election, and how it must affect my plans. Yet I must be peculiarly constituted. The tighter the quarters I get into, the calmer and cooler I become. I don't think that is usually the case with men of large affairs. But I am not seeking power, glory or anything of that kind. I have only one fixed purpose—to be freed from my creditors."

But he would be free honorably.

By now the *Times* circulation was climbing past 25,000 and its columns were carrying more general advertising than they had in the past fifteen years. By appealing to the intelligent reader, Ochs was pulling his newspaper slowly and steadily uphill. Now red ink was used most sparingly in the auditing department, and if it were not for Ochs's insistence on spending a little more every month to improve news coverage and the appearance of the paper, that red-ink bottle would long have been tossed into the trash bin. Because he kept plowing every possible cent into bettering his paper, the *Times* was still teetering on the brink of breaking even.

One day an astonishing proposition was made to him. A lawyer named Samuel Untermeyer visited Ochs in his office.

"I am empowered to offer you a most favorable arrangement," Untermeyer said. "I hope you will give it serious consideration."

Ochs sat back and listened.

Untermeyer had come as an emissary from Tammany Hall. The men in power there did not understand a man like Adolph Ochs. If he had raised a fuss about sharing city advertising with other newspapers, claiming it was unnecessary for the ads to appear in more than one paper, they reasoned that he must think the *Times* ought to be the sole chosen paper. Why not make a deal with him? So they authorized Untermeyer to offer him the city's entire, juicy, $200,000 advertising contract for the coming year.

"And what would Tammany want in return?" Ochs asked coolly.

Untermeyer hedged at first, insisting that of course the *Times* was not being bought and that its complete independence would always be respected. No special favors would be asked in return for the lucrative contract. Nothing important, that is. Right at the moment there was "a certain millionaire newspaperman," not otherwise identified, who longed to work for *The New York Times*. If he were put on the payroll at $10,000 a year, he and the *Times* both would benefit.

There was nothing illegal about the Tammany offer. The city did indeed have the legal duty to advertise for bids in one or another newspaper of general circulation. At the moment Ochs desperately needed $200,000, but he would not play ball with Tammany. In no uncertain terms he made his position quite clear.

"Untermeyer kept urging me to accept the offer," Ochs told Effie later. "He thinks I am supersensitive and that I lean over backwards in these matters, but in his heart he must believe that I am right. I will enter into no understanding with Tammany."

Standing on principle was a luxury he could not afford, but Ochs did it anyhow. And, a few months later, his paper overtook the *Tribune* in advertising revenue. It gained circulation steadily, and it attracted favorable comment among editors all over the country. But Ochs was by no means out of the financial woods yet.

He worked sixteen hours every day, pruning away at waste and going over every paragraph that appeared in the paper. To take some of the burden from his own shoulders, he brought his trusted cousin, Ben Franck, up from Chattanooga as confidential assistant, the same cousin whose elegant overcoat he had ruined during the Grover Cleveland parade. Franck proved a big help, and a cheerful gadfly, too. One midnight when Ochs wearily stopped at his desk after a long session in the composing room, he found this jingle written by Franck:

> I am the Boss
> The Editor bold
> And the Chief of
> The New York Times
> The Big Ad Man,
> The Office Boy,
> And he Who handles
> The Dimes.

Ochs laughed, then took the hint. He left for home, instead of staying around another hour or two. Home now was in an apartment in the noisy, cheerful house of a tea taster friend, Thomas Read, who had six young children, one boy just Baby's age. Having grown up in a house filled with children, Ochs wanted his daughter to have the same happy, exciting kind of childhood to look back on. If Effie preferred a less boisterous atmosphere she never said so. Dolph's gusto and energy still astonished her, but she had learned to take them in stride, along with the domestic uproar he liked.

The two years the Ochs family spent with the Reads were crucial years for Adolph Ochs and his newspaper. Late in 1897, to cap all his other troubles, his main source of out-of-city news collapsed. This was the old United Press, forerunner of the later wire service bearing the same name. The old UP was serving four major morning newspapers in New York when it folded—the *Sun*, the *Herald*, the *Tribune* and the *Times*. Suddenly all four papers faced the urgent need for membership in the only other general wire news service then operating, the Associated Press.

But the AP then was organized something like a club and applications for membership could be vetoed by an existing member in the same city. As the major morning newspaper publisher already holding an AP franchise, Joseph Pulitzer found himself in a delightfully powerful position. He had the right to veto any or all of the four new applications—and he used it. He turned down the application of *The New York Times*.

Why would he waive his veto in three cases, then use it in the fourth? An eccentric genius, Pulitzer never explained his action, but it probably was based on cold logic. He was shrewd enough to know that vetoing all four applications would surely cause the kind of court appeal that later, in Chicago, did end the monopolistic practice of limiting AP membership this way. But why did he single out the *Times*? Very probably because he understood more clearly than anyone else that Ochs was his only serious threat. Although Pulitzer was slashing into the New York newspaper field by sensational tactics, he had a plan in mind; eventually he planned to make the *World* as sound a newspaper as his St. Louis *Post-Dispatch* and then the *Times* could be dangerous competition.

To admit this publicly would have been absurd, for the *Times* was still a weak sister beside the rich and popular *World*. So Pulitzer admitted nothing. He merely stood firm in his vote against the *Times,* till a chorus of protest caused him to relent a bit.

Ochs already had many friends in the newspaper world. As publisher of the Chattanooga *Times*, he had long been a member of the southern AP, and leaders of the agency there did some powerful lobbying for him. Grudgingly, Pulitzer finally voted to grant *The New York Times* a Class B membership in the AP, which entitled Ochs to a limited budget of news. The restriction was removed a few years later, after the Chicago court decree caused reorganization of the AP, but even with a limited membership Ochs could breathe easier for the time being.

Not for long, though. Much worse trouble lay just around the corner.

Despite all he said about not aiming to compete with Hearst and Pulitzer, he suddenly found himself forced by circumstances beyond his control to compete—or give up. The cruel choice was forced on him by the Spanish-American War.

The theory that the war hysteria of 1898 was coldbloodedly whipped up in the columns of the *World* and *Journal* as a cynical circulation-building stunt has been advanced by some historians. Wherever the truth lies, there is no doubt that "Willie" Hearst leaped into the quarrel that was developing between Spain and the United States over Cuba and printed screaming headlines not calculated to soothe away the trouble. Pulitzer whooped almost as loud. And their circulation rocketed upward.

But the staid *New York Times*, which was urging caution on President McKinley, began to lose readers.

Late in January of 1898, the United States Navy sent its battleship, the *Maine*, to Havana harbor to protect American interests in seething Cuba. When the Maine mysteriously blew up, killing 266 American sailors, there was hardly an American who believed Spanish protestations of innocence in the matter. War was declared. Even the careful, sensible *Times* had to face the fact that war news was big news now.

Every word about the conflict found avid readers, and newspapers embarked on a fantastic orgy of money-spending. Even lesser papers in New York like the *Herald* joined in with a vengeance; the *Herald* printed a 2,000-word scoop about the destruction of the Spanish fleet, sent by urgent cable, via Panama, at a cost of $3.25 a word, paid for on the spot with a sack of gold. The *World* and the *Journal* hired launches for their correspondents, who cabled back tingling, eyewitness stories that sold papers by the stack. Ochs had no cash for any such grandiose exploits, and could print only straight AP news. As a result, he lost readers every week.

He did some sober calculating when the short, swift war ended. He was selling only about 25,000 papers a day. To keep the *Times* going another year, he would have to double his readership in a few short months, or admit defeat.

Ochs could not even think of defeat. He would find a way out, he had to!

Casting about for an idea, he hit on a dramatic plan that every single adviser warned him against. As a desperate gamble, he slashed the price of *The New York Times* early in October to one penny a copy.

Like other respectable newspapers throughout the nation, the *Times* had been selling for three cents. The price of a newspaper had huge implications in those days. The penny press meant squalid sheets with no pretension towards journalistic purity; two-cent papers were a bit more respectable; but papers that made their appeal to the solid citizenry showed their superior status by charging three cents.

"It is the price of the paper, not its character, that will change," Ochs insisted. He argued that the price cut would increase readership among teachers and others who might prefer a substantial newspaper but could not afford it.

Arguing against him, friends and associates held out for the traditional view that anyone interested in a daily appealing to intelligence, rather than emotion, could well afford the slight extra expense.

"Men who want the *Times* would pay three cents as soon as one," a trade magazine called the *Journalist* contended. "The circulation won't increase one little bit." But Ochs thought he knew better. In barber shops he had seen well-dressed businessmen reading the *Journal,* and if there were some among the prosperous who could enjoy a paper stressing entertainment, why couldn't there be some among the less prosperous who craved solid news?

Newspapers all over the United States wrote scoffing editorials about the *Times* price change. "The spectacle of the staid and respectable old *Times* trying to compete with the *World* and *Journal* is enough to make the ghosts of Henry J. Raymond and George Jones go tearing down Broadway in their war chariots," the Buffalo *Express* fumed. But within one month, Adolph Ochs proved who was right. The quality of *The New York Times* had not suffered in the least and its circulation had started to spurt upward.

Circulation of the *Times* had been 25,726 on October 10, 1898, when the price cut took effect. One year later to the day, the circulation manager took quite a different figure from a folder in his roll-top desk. On October 10, 1899, *The New York Times* sold 76,260 copies!

And this leap in circulation did not tell the whole story. No newspaper's price, then or now, even pays for the rolls of blank newsprint it threads into its presses. It is from advertising that a newspaper pays its bills and perhaps makes a profit, and advertising is measured in lines. Now, in one year, the *Times* had picked up almost 1,000,000 lines of new advertising, attracted by its soaring circulation. The auditor's bottle of red ink went out the window. Adolph Ochs and his *New York Times* were on their way!

10

A most important technicality still remained to be settled. When Ochs had worked his spell on Spencer Trask back in 1896, the agreement arrived at by the financier and the publisher contained this proviso: Ochs would have to make *The New York Times* pay its way for three consecutive years before he took full, legal control of the newspaper. All the money Ochs had been able to raise in 1896 to buy stock in his own name had been a mere $75,000—paltry in terms of an enterprise like a big metropolitan newspaper, but a fabulously large sum for a near-bankrupt southern stranger. With only $75,000 in stock, Ochs could not control the New York Times Company. But a big block of additional stock was being held for him in a bank vault. If he made good on his promise to revive the *Times*, he would get this as a reward, and thenceforth have a clear majority of outstanding stock. Then he would indisputably be the boss.

On the fourteenth of August in 1900, exactly four years after taking over on Park Row, Ochs was presented with the promised stock certificates. *The New York Times* was truly his now. "The deed is done!" he told Effie.

And what a deed it was! In 1900, the circulation of the *Times* reached 82,000, and advertising was climbing every month. From an investment of only $75,000, Ochs had stock certificates now worth well over $1,000,000. This was no dream, but cold, financial fact; in 1900, he had several offers for his interest in the paper, and one offer was for *$2,000,000*. But Ochs was not selling. With his own toil and sweat, he had put *The New York Times* back in the first rank of American newspapers, and now he hoped to push it even further.

"I would not sell now for ten million dollars," he said. "I want to prove that what I have done here is only the bare start. When I have completed my work, ten million will seem trifling."

He had no wish to rival Carnegie and Rockefeller and the other fabulous rags-to-riches men who were assembling immense fortunes then. As the principal stockholder of a thriving New York daily, Ochs could expect a handsome income from now on; indeed, the mere transfer of the withheld stock had made him a rich man, and he could easily pay off every last penny he owed in Chattanooga and in New York. But money for its own sake did not interest him, comforting as it was to be debt-free at last and to be able to take excellent care of his family. What did interest him was the challenge of publishing a gem of a newspaper the likes of which no publisher had ever before achieved.

Since his boyhood in Knoxville, when he had had his first sniff of pungent printer's ink, he had not doubted that someday he would have a newspaper of his own. At twenty, starting to build the Chattanooga *Times*, he had known exactly what kind of a newspaper he wanted. At thirty-eight, taking over *The New York Times*, he had worked tirelessly to adapt his tested formula to the nation's biggest city. Now, at forty-two, at the height of his powers and unhampered for the first time in his life by money problems, he could reach for the very top of his profession.

He had a simple formula, deceptively simple. To print all the news, as completely and accurately and attractively as possible, did not sound a bit revolutionary; a number of other publishers had come up with the same formula. But in one way or another these publishers usually compromised. "You have to be realistic," they said in self-justification. "You can't make a paper pay in this town if you don't play ball with City Hall." Or, "You can't insult a big department store family." Or, "What's the sense of wasting space on a boring tax meeting when people want to read about that red-headed typist who ran off with her boss?" Adolph Ochs would not stoop to such compromise.

But human frailty being what it is, where did he find a staff of supermen? Men who would judge news on its merits alone, who would write unbiased stories about Candidate A and Candidate B, too? The answer is that the woods were and are full of newspaper men and women with ideals, anxious to work for a decent boss who will stand up for them in a dispute with an aggrieved reader. If a reporter or an editor knows his boss is fair and honest, the chances are excellent that the reporter or editor will do his own work fairly and honestly. Or so Adolph Ochs found.

"The thing I'm proudest of," he told Effie, "is making a success of the paper with the same men who had worked there when it was a failure."

Like the conductor of a great symphony orchestra, Ochs could and did draw magic from the minds and fingers of other men and women with the same high ideals and passion for honesty that motivated him.

People were beginning to call him a genius, but Ochs shrugged off any such fancy label. In his own eyes he was just a lucky man with good common sense. "I do not understand the tributes that come my way," he wrote to a friend. "I have merely proved that, given the chance, the reading public will choose a newspaper that serves up the news without coloring. I knew it would work out that way."

But it took more than good sense and a little luck to put *The New York Times* on the upward track towards which it raced in 1900. It took ceaseless attention to detail; it took a lightning quick mind; it took far-sighted vision and understanding of the potentialities of the new inventions that were popping up everywhere and drastically changing the whole American scene. Telephones, typewriters, radio telegraphy would have a profound effect on newspapering. Ochs was among the first to see the opportunities these presented for gathering more news, faster than ever before. Ochs saw, too, that by taking advantage of every innovation, it would be possible to print a newspaper of unparalleled completeness.

There had been only two telephones in the *Times* office when Ochs took over—one linking the city desk with the reporters' room at police headquarters, and one in the advertising department. Now he put in more, as fast as he could pay for them. He bought typewriters and replaced the old slant-top desks at which reporters had stood scrawling their stories by hand. Although old-timers protested at first, it soon became obvious that the change resulted in quicker, clearer stories.

Not only was he a lucky man with a good head on his shoulders; Ochs was also living at the right time and in the right place to make journalistic history.

Already, in 1900, the horizon of his planning for his *New York Times* stretched far beyond mere competition with other New York newspapers. That year he brought his brother George up from Chattanooga and gave him a thrilling assignment.

"I want you to go to Paris," he told him. There was to be a great international exposition in the French capital that summer. "I want you to put out a *New York Times* on the exposition grounds every day this summer. *The New York Times* already is well known in Europe, but this will make it even better known. The *Times* will be the only newspaper printed at the exposition. People from all corners of the world will visit the fair grounds. When they leave, they will have a better idea of how we work here in New York."

So George hired 1,500 square feet in the American pavilion at the fair, paid $50,000 for linotype machines and a big press, and behind a huge plate-glass window printed 20,000 copies every day of a fourteen-page newspaper modeled on its parent paper across the ocean. French newspapers ran to only six to eight pages. White-bearded King Leopold of Belgium was among the fascinated visitors who pressed their noses against the plate glass to watch the giant American press pounding out newspapers.

As an advertising gimmick, the Paris edition was a magnificent success, and for his spectacular sideshow George got a medal from the French government. Brother Adolph, who had paid the bills, was overlooked when the medals were awarded but he didn't mind. The fun he and Effie had on their first trip abroad on a brief summer holiday made up for this small slight.

In Europe, as at home, Ochs found himself something of a celebrity. He and Effie were invited to splendid mansions and treated with deference by distinguished hosts. As the publisher of an increasingly powerful newspaper, Ochs was becoming a power to be cultivated. But instead of turning pompous, Ochs now began to relax.

He sneaked off to the horse races whenever he could; he went to the theatre; he played the jovial host himself at lively dinner parties where the food and wine were excellent. Lobster with a splendid French sauce, or juicy watermelon at a Fourth of July picnic, were eaten with gusto. As a boy he had been too poor for feasting and too busy to play; now he was making up for lost time.

Back home, which was now a handsome West Side house of his own, he lived stylishly, with a Swiss governess for Baby. Almost every evening, he turned up laden with toys and he spent time romping with his daughter, whom he adored. And now that he could afford to indulge a long-stifled yen for fine clothes, he hired a tailor just for the luxury of having a suit made to his own measurements. "Paid $75 at Rock's in Fifth Avenue for a new suit," he wrote to his mother. "Not bad for a country greenie from Tennessee, eh?"

By now he was extremely well off, yet he did not forget his less-elegant past. When his mother wrote that the old Knoxville neighbor who had once given him a pair of hand-me-down pants was now a penniless widow, he instructed his auditor at the *Times* to send her a monthly check. She was to live for many years, but every month she got her check. "That was one of the most expensive pairs of pants in history," the auditor told Ochs wryly. Ochs smiled, but kept paying till the woman died.

Another old tie with Knoxville cropped up in 1900, and he wrote his mother, "I had a visit from Miss Frances Humes, daughter of the late Dr. Thomas W. Humes of Knoxville. She is eking out an existence as a fashionable dressmaker. She contemplates a trip to Paris, and wishes to write a few fashion letters for the *Times*. I told her we would be overjoyed to have them."

The Dr. Humes to whom he referred had been the president of the Knoxville school Ochs had quit at fifteen.

Rummaging in his desk at home, he found an old brown leather album in which, so many years ago, he had pasted a beautifully penned letter.

> Adolph Ochs was until the summer of 1873 a pupil in my school. His application to study, and his general demeanor were very satisfactory and creditable to him. . . . I cordially recommend him to the kind regard and friendly attention of all persons of worth and influence, wherever he may go.

This was signed Thomas W. Humes.

Miss Humes's visit triggered another idea, and Ochs thoughtfully drafted a letter to the manager of the *Times* of London, to explore the possibilities for some sort of cooperative news-pooling scheme between that august journal and his own *New York Times*.

For a few months, negotiations were conducted via transatlantic mail. Ochs, who was putting together probably the best news-gathering machinery on his side of the ocean, proposed to supply American news to the London paper, in exchange for its European dispatches. Several tentative plans, even one calling for joint publication of an

International Times in Paris, were thoroughly aired, then finally dropped. On second thought, Ochs decided against forming close ties with the London daily which was the semi-official mouthpiece for the British government and spoke openly for the government on foreign affairs. He felt he could not risk having his *New York Times* branded as a tool of British interests. However, he did buy and print a limited amount of London *Times* news for many years.

And still his head was filled with other spectacular new plans.

11

The Park Row plant of *The New York Times* far from satis-fied Ochs. Since the fateful day when he had first stepped into its front office, he had put every penny he could spare into makeshift improvements, but the musty old building over-looking City Hall Park could not begin to fill his idea of a suit-able home for his newspaper. It was too small and dingy. It lacked space for all the men and machines he needed to print all the news. Now his vague longing to build a bold new land-mark that would make a fitting home for the *Times* began assuming more solid proportions.

In 1901, circulation leaped to 102,000, and with all these new readers came new advertising—almost 5,000,000 lines for the year, compared with half that amount in 1896. Now Ochs felt he could afford to start looking for something spe-cial in the way of real estate.

He had the money for it, and he also had the matchless elation that comes with seeing a dream come true. He had every hope of reaching even greater heights. Why not, with a staff like his?

His own spirit of high journalistic adventure was shared by all his men, down to the lowly office boy. At two o'clock on the morning of September 13, 1901, the *Times* newsroom had finally emptied after a long, hard night. President McKinley had been shot that day by a half-crazed anarchist while he was inspecting the Pan-American Exposition up in Buffalo, New York, and the first reports had said the President was critically injured. Then, in the evening, doctors had announced he was rallying. Satisfied at last that the *Times* had the story nailed down, managing editor Henry Loewenthal sent everybody home. Only Tommy Bracken, the night office boy, was left, doggedly typing out a feature story he hoped to get into the Sunday paper.

At three o'clock, Tommy was still typing away when he heard the thump of a message arriving in the pneumatic tube from the Associated Press. The boy knew nobody would see the message till morning. Curious about why the AP was sending a bulletin to a morning paper at this hour, he rose and unwrapped it.

"PRESIDENT MCKINLEY IS SINKING," he read.

A timid lad, Tommy hesitated. Then, fingers quivering, he took the bulletin and hurried down to the composing room. There he found an assistant foreman still on duty, minding the press that was clattering out more copies of *The New York Times* telling the world the President was resting comfortably after his injury.

"The *Times* will look silly," Tommy insisted. "We have to do something."

The assistant foreman threw a switch that stopped the press.

From nearby saloons, a skeleton crew of printers was dragged back, and for the next three hours young Tommy Bracken feverishly pasted up AP bulletins, and printers set up new type, and somehow replated the front page. Three separate new editions of *The New York Times* were printed this way, reporting first that McKinley was dying, then that Cabinet members were being summoned to his bedside and finally that Vice President Theodore Roosevelt would soon take over as President of the United States.

The sun had risen when Tommy trudged home to sleep. Newsboys were shouting, "Extra! Extra!" and waving copies of his newspaper. Terrified at his own boldness, the boy could hardly sleep, and by noon was fearfully stepping back into the dingy newsroom. Loewenthal shouted for him at once.

"Who wrote this headline?" the managing editor demanded sharply, pointing to a late edition of the *Times* on his desk.

Tommy swallowed. "I did," he said weakly.

"Why did *you* write it? Where was everybody?"

Loewenthal listened without a word as the lad told him what had happened, then nodded and waved him away. Tommy hurried off, relieved. An hour later, Loewenthal posted a notice on the bulletin board:

"I take this opportunity publicly to express my appreciation of the work of Mr. Thomas Bracken, who, alone and unaided, this morning got out the third, fourth and fifth editions."

Then Tommy was summoned to the publisher's office. From Ochs he got a shiny twenty-dollar gold piece for his night's work. Tommy Bracken spent fifty-five years on the staff of *The New York Times*, the last several years as boss of the newspaper's huge morgue, or clipping library.

With loyalty like this, Ochs felt confident of the future. Late in 1901 he made up his mind to build—and build monumentally.

After dinner on December 31, just before a new year would be ushered in, he swooped his seven-year-old daughter out of bed, got her dressed in her warmest clothes and took her by horsecab all the way down snowy Broadway to Park Row.

Baby had been at the office many times in daylight, for Ochs enjoyed having her trail beside him, her hand clutching his, as he bustled through the building. As a matter of fact, he often took her to the theatre, to lectures, to all sorts of fascinating penny shows and not such fascinating grown-up meetings, but this was the first time she had been taken down to the office at night.

At half-past eleven, Ochs led his daughter to a window overlooking City Hall Park. A crowd of people, gathered on the snowy grass, were blowing raucously on tin horns and jangling cowbells. In those days New Year's Eve brought out great festive mobs, and this was a very special New Year's Eve. City Hall itself was outlined with glowing red, white and blue electric lights, and printers were ready atop the *Times* building and other newspaper buildings in the area to greet the new century with gaudy fireworks.

"Every hundred years makes a new century," Ochs told his daughter. "Tonight the people of this city, and of cities all over the world, will assemble in crowds as they have here in City Hall Park. They will say farewell to the nineteenth century, and they will welcome in the twentieth century. It is an unusual event. No person shall ever see two such celebrations. I brought you here tonight to watch. It is something you will always remember."

Church chimes began to strike midnight and suddenly the crowd grew silent. Tin horns and brass bands hushed. The lights on City Hall went out. Then a wild, exultant sound arose again as lights flashed back to jewel brightness across the face of City Hall, spelling out: "Welcome Twentieth Century!" Golden sparks from the printers' fireworks floated down past the window Ochs and his daughter were staring through, and from the harbor, ships boomed their salute.

The spell of the moment caught Ochs. Hugging Baby, he promised himself that in the new century *The New York Times* would have a new home befitting its dignity, a building worthy of its position as the greatest newspaper in the great and growing city of New York.

Traditionally, newspapers were published downtown then, in the cramped, narrow streets and old-fashioned squares of nineteenth-century lower Manhattan. The retail trade had moved uptown already, and fashionable brownstone residences were starting to line streets that not too long ago had been part of country estates near Central Park.

"I would like a good site uptown," Ochs told his lawyer and friend Leopold Wallach late in 1901. "Preferably, one where the building can be seen from a distance of several blocks."

The simple grid pattern on which the newer New York streets were laid out posed a problem, for there were few wide squares uptown where a building would be visible for blocks around. But a mere corner plot would not satisfy

Ochs; he had to have an eye-catching location on a broad and busy square.

There were only a few possibilities—at the squares formed where independent Broadway, wandering uptown along its old, colonial path, intersected another main north-south avenue. Ochs set his heart first on a site on the square formed where Broadway and Fifth Avenue came together at Twenty-third Street—Madison Square, where he already had his "All the News That's Fit to Print" sign. Not knowing whom to deal with first, he approached his friend Henry Morgenthau, a power in the New York real estate field.

"I want to buy on Madison Square," Ochs told him. "Who controls the land?"

"I do," Morgenthau said. Then smiling, he explained that he was the broker for the owners, who were anxious to sell. "But don't buy land there," he advised, giving up a handsome commission for the sake of friendship. The heyday of Madison Square was already passing, he explained, and the place to buy was further north, where Broadway and Seventh Avenue came together at Forty-second Street. This intersection was then called Longacre Square. Ochs took his friend's advice and began to seek property there.

When it became known that Ochs proposed to build a newspaper office that far uptown, there was head-shaking in other newspaper plants. How could a paper be produced—and delivered—from such an out-of-the-way spot? Other publishers said it couldn't be done. Certainly it had never been done before. Till then, the bulk of the city's activity had been well below Fifty-ninth Street, and horse-drawn wagons lumbered through narrow downtown streets to make deliveries in a comparatively small radius. Now the city was swiftly spreading uptown, however, and the new underground subway trains could take stacks of paper further and faster than ever before.

At last, Ochs got title to a triangular island of ground between Broadway and Seventh Avenue at Forty-second Street. A rundown hotel then occupied most of this site.

News that Ochs planned to build there had caused much comment, but news of *what* he planned to build created even more excitement. To make the best of an unusually shaped plot, open to view on every side, the architects Ochs hired designed one of New York's most unusual buildings—a 362-foot tower inspired by Giotto's famous bell tower in Florence, Italy. The Times Tower would rise twenty-four stories, dwarfing every other building in the area. Over the roofs of its much lower neighbors, it would be visible from Madison Square, from Central Park, from ships steaming into New York harbor. And the Times Tower would have a further distinction. Because it would rise right on top of the tracks of the new West Side subway being constructed, and because a huge basement was needed for the paper's immense presses, this tower also plunged unbelievably deep into the ground.

In 1903, when workmen in hip boots began damming underground streams to start the foundation, every newspaper in the city carried stories about "the deepest hole in town." Newspapers and magazines throughout Europe printed excited articles describing *The New York Times*'s skyscraper, which would be Manhattan's and the world's second tallest building. The first, which was only a few feet taller, was a downtown office structure, since demolished.

"DEEPEST HOLE IN NEW YORK A BROADWAY SPECTACLE," James Gordon Bennett's *Herald* informed its readers.

> The excavation is highly interesting by night. The brilliant illumination of Broadway (already a theatre center) reaches to the well-like depths of the great shaft. The jagged rocks stand out in striking relief against the shadows. The great throng which surges along the brightly illuminated sidewalks of Broadway looks down at an abrupt angle into what appears to be a bottomless abyss. . . .

In all of this picturesque prose, the *Herald* writer neglected one fact. Possibly on orders from the eccentric Bennett, who would not cheerfully applaud the achievement of another publisher, not once in the article was there mention of *The New York Times* or Adolph Ochs. But all New York knew who was putting up this extraordinary building.

Despite storms and floods and the incredible complication of working around and above subway construction, work on the Times Tower went forward. One snarl after another had to be somehow untangled. Ochs once teased his lawyer, Leopold Wallach. "You're not objecting to anything today," Ochs said. "You're agreeing too easily. Why?"

"Well, Adolph," Wallach said, "if you must know, I approve because you are never happy except when you are in hot water, and this project will keep you in hot water for the rest of your life."

Ochs's family, by now, had somewhat the same attitude. Effie had long since decided that her husband was a great man who needed the challenge of great projects, but some of the others took a slightly less tolerant view. Writing to his mother, Ochs noted placidly: "George is afraid that after all my newspaper schemes are exhausted I will start to plan a road to the moon, or some such visionary enterprise. I pass it along in anticipation of what he may say when he gets back to Chattanooga."

On January 18, 1904, the cornerstone of the Times Tower was finally set in place. The frame went up quickly after that, and a few months later, when Ochs sailed for another European jaunt, he wrote to his mother from aboard ship a few minutes after leaving land:

> The new building loomed up in all its beautiful and grand proportions, out of mid-New York, as we sailed away, and my heart swelled as I thought of my association with its erection. Then it stood foremost and most conspicuous among the best buildings in the Metropolis of the World— and I really grew sentimental.
>
> It is a beauty, and even though the $2,500,000 that went into it cost some anxieties, it is there and it will be a monument to one man's daring.

As a monument and as a magnet for crowds, the Times Tower was an immediate standout success. Shortly after the newspaper moved in, early in 1905, a ribbon of electric-light news bulletins began to travel around its facade, and for many years every great event in human history drew hundreds of thousands of New Yorkers to stare up at the moving sign.

No less appreciative than Chattanooga had been years earlier, New York thanked Adolph Ochs for his spectacular civic ornament by changing the name of Longacre Square to Times Square.

A man of great consequence now, the owner of the Times Tower had a touching experience during one of his now frequent European tours. While in Germany, he was summoned to a health spa to spend a week with his old enemy, Joseph Pulitzer. Ochs wrote home:

> He is a remarkable man, a man of great strength and great intellectual power, and of education and culture. His success has not been accidental. He is a man among thousands. It is a great and tragic misfortune that he is virtually blind. If he had not that affliction he would be a tremendous figure in national affairs. He told me that he is an invalid, that he suffers continuously from severe headaches, and that he is extremely nervous. He is so nervous that he objected to the scraping of the brakes on the carriage wheels. He has to have such quiet that he takes a whole villa for himself. He was very cordial, and very complimentary to *The New York Times*. He spoke disparagingly of his own New York *World*.

The day Pulitzer must have foreseen had now arrived. His own *World*, sobered down and a fine newspaper, was meeting increasingly stiff competition from that former weak sister, the *Times*. Broken in health, Pulitzer could see trouble ahead for his own newspaper, but after all he was a big enough man to bury his old bitterness toward Ochs.

Ochs took time now for gay, reviving vacations, not only in Europe, but in his own country. Usually, in addition to his own family, he brought along a whole party of nieces and nephews and cousins. And by now, at her own insistence, his daughter was called Iphigene or Iffy because she felt much too grown-up to be Baby any more. In the summer of 1904, only a year after the first cross-country automobile trip had gone into the record books, Ochs bought a secondhand

Mercedes from one of his editors and took his family on a pioneering ride through New England.

The Mercedes was an open car, and it could not be closed no matter what the weather. Everybody, child and adult alike, wore a long, loose coat, called a duster, and a pair of goggles, as some slight protection from the dust of the rural lanes that were the only roads then. A rubber sheet covered the baggage tied to the rear.

Singing off-key at the top of his lungs, for he could not carry a tune to save his life, Ochs conducted his family as far north as Canada. As they were bumping up a cowpath into Maine, a weather-beaten Yankee farmer called out, "What do you call that thing you're in?" It was the first time he had seen a horseless carriage.

On light-hearted vacation, Ochs was always on the look-out for a chance to play a joke. Driving through Cape Cod, he was warned at one of the rare filling stations that the next town was a speed trap, and anyone riding through it at more than six miles an hour would be arrested. The local constable had tied a bell to a string across the only road and as soon as an approaching car ran over the string, thus causing the bell to peal, he took out his watch to begin timing the car's progress.

Forewarned, Ochs drove slowly through the town—backwards. He thought this a fine way to poke fun at the suspicious constable. And just in case the first peal of the bell, as he backed over the string, should have been missed, Ochs had his young nephew Julius Ochs Adler walk alongside the backward-creeping car, carrying the tolling bell at the end of its string.

"Julie" Adler, who later became a general in the United States Army as well as a high executive at *The New York*

Times, was mortified at having to take part in the practical joke. His uncle, though, thoroughly enjoyed the constable's confusion—and the fact that the party got through the town without paying a fine.

Even on his vacation trips, Ochs kept part of his mind on his work. He read local papers carefully; he kept his eyes alert going through small manufacturing towns. He asked questions about *New York Times* distribution in cities along his route. Once his identity was known, he was treated royally, but more often than not his identity did not become known. After his one brash public performance, marching in the sound-money parade during the McKinley campaign, Ochs increasingly avoided ceremony at home and abroad. As much as possible, he delegated his charming business manager, Louis Wiley, to appear for him at receptions and speech-making occasions, while he stayed well behind the scenes.

There were comparatively few interviews with him or articles about him, except in certain journalistic trade papers. This was true despite the eminence his paper was attaining. The day of the colorful publisher, who used his newspaper mainly as an extension of his own personality, had begun to fade fast—and Ochs approved of the change. His own *Times*, in fact, had done much to hasten the process of making the publisher a quiet influence in the wings, rather than a ranting, outspoken character in stage center, and he personally was more comfortable out of the limelight.

That he had become an important man, a powerful man, cannot be denied, though. As the active director of a newspaper with the prestige of *The New York Times*, the situation could not be otherwise. Top men in government and finance understood how important Ochs was, even if the general reader did not, for he could make or break a man by causing a particular story to be printed—or not printed—in his newspaper.

Ochs understood this himself. But when he rambled on to Effie about building a newspaper that would be a respected institution beyond personal considerations, he meant what he said. When he went overboard financially to build a splendid new building fitting the dignity of *The New York Times*, he truly believed that his newspaper deserved this distinction. He thought it merited a special status that no person, even himself, could tamper with, that his paper was a public trust. He felt he owed it to his readers to keep the *Times* above suspicion.

So although he associated with the rich and the powerful more and more as time went on, he made it clear always that he would not compromise his newspaper. Only once did his secretary ever hear him lose his temper, and this blow-up resulted from a telephone call Ochs had from a banker friend. There was an investigation in progress at the time, of scandals involving some important Wall Street names. "Don't you owe it to us to keep this unsavory stuff out of the *Times*?" Ochs was asked.

"The *Times* owes you nothing!" Ochs exploded.

To make sure the point would be plain, Ochs decided early in his New York days that he must not repeat one set of Chattanooga mistakes. Never again would he dabble in other business and risk the good name of *The New York Times*.

When railroad stock deals were coming thick and fast, Ochs murmured over a page of proofs to his cousin, Ben Franck: "Do you know, Ben, I could have made over a million dollars this week on that railroad deal. I was tipped off to what was going to happen."

"Then why didn't you?" Franck demanded.

"When I came to New York, Ben, I pledged myself never to dabble in Wall Street," Ochs answered quietly. "I knew I would have to give all my time to making a success of the *Times*. I swore I'd concentrate on that."

12

Back in 1901 Guglielmo Marconi had signaled the letter "S" across the Atlantic Ocean, from England to Newfoundland—by wireless. Ochs had grasped the significance of wireless at once. Picking a new managing editor for *The New York Times* in 1904, the publisher made sure of getting a man who shared his own appreciation of the news-gathering possibilities of this marvelous invention. From the staff of the *Sun*, Ochs plucked forty-year-old Carr Van Anda, one of the best management choices of his entire career.

Very shortly after coming to the *Times*, Van Anda showed Ochs that he knew how to use infant wireless spectacularly. The Russo-Japanese War of 1904-5 was proving far more difficult to cover than the Spanish-American War earlier, despite the vast change in the financial position of the *Times*, because the fighting was taking place at sea off Siberia, halfway around the world from New York, and conventional cable dispatches could not be sent easily. Correspondents had to find a cable office first, and by the time their messages arrived the news was days old. Van Anda thought of a better way.

He suggested that the *Times* hire a steamer in the Far East and equip it with a wireless transmitter—and Ochs gleefully agreed to the expense, which he arranged to share with the London *Times*. Then, as opposing naval forces were building up for a great battle off Port Arthur, in New York Van Anda and Ochs waited tensely.

On the morning of April 14, 1904, a copy boy approached them with the first page of a story that had just crackled into the office headed:

OFF PORT ARTHUR, ON BOARD THE TIMES STEAMSHIP HAIMUN, APRIL 13, JAPANESE TORPEDO CRAFT ATTACKED PORT ARTHUR EARLY THIS MORNING AND THE FLEET SHELLED THE PORT . . . .

There followed the complete story of the engagement, the first story ever to be sent to a newspaper from a ship at sea. Transmission technicalities were still such that the words had been radioed only as far as a Chinese port, and from there cabled first to London, then from London to New York. But a brand-new era in journalism had begun.

Ochs authorized Van Anda to blow the *Times*'s own horn about its beat. The wireless story ran under a comparatively sedate headline, "TORPEDO ATTACK YESTERDAY," but then italics told how the scoop had been scored. When other New York newspapers, awaiting conventional cables, shamelessly cribbed from the *Times* dispatch, the next day Ochs printed an editorial: "A Warning." This explained the magic of wireless and rapped the knuckles of other editors who had merely copied what had appeared in his own paper.

"It is absolutely from out at sea that the *Times* steamship *Haimun* is able to relieve the anxiety of a waiting world by sending the results of ocular observation of a sea fight between Russia and Japan," the editorial said sternly.

Not only were other newspapers thrown into confusion by *The New York Times* feat, but high Russian diplomats protested the *Times* had been guilty of spying and threatened to have the Russian navy seize the *Haimun*. Despite much aggrieved muttering, the threat was not carried out.

A driving perfectionist, Van Anda quickly endeared himself to his boss by coups like this, and Ochs soon left much of the day-to-day operation of *The New York Times* in his hands. The two men thought alike about newspapering; there was never any danger of sloppy, irresponsible journalism with Van Anda striding up and down the newsroom. In the business departments, too, Ochs chose good men, then let them do their jobs with only gentle supervision. Though he could never give up his own ceaseless concern about the *Times*, extending even to filing the edge of an offending piece of metal type when he bustled through the composing room, he was not the publisher to shower petty orders on his staff. When he was away on trips, he knew his men could cope with any crisis that came up, for he had picked only men he could trust.

Van Anda redoubled Ochs's admiration by his handling of the last and biggest battle of the Russo-Japanese War. For days a decisive engagement had been expected, and the managing editor kept a skeleton crew on tap till dawn lest the story be delayed a single unnecessary second in reaching print. Tense and sleepless, he was pacing the newsroom at 4:31 A.M. on May 29, 1905, when a boy handed him the flash:

TOKYO, MAY 29, 2:15 P.M., IT IS OFFICIALLY ANNOUNCED THAT ADMIRAL ROJESTVENSKY'S FLEET HAS BEEN ANNIHILATED. . . .

Van Anda sprang into action. After swiftly reading the copy, with his own pencil he boldly wrote the following headlines:

TOGO SMASHES
RUSSIAN FLEET

TOKYO ANNOUNCES 12 SHIPS
SUNK OR CAPTURED

---

2 TRANSPORTS DESTROYED

---

2 TORPEDO BOAT DESTROYERS
SENT TO BOTTOM

JAPANESE CRUISER LOST

TEN TORPEDO BOATS ARE
ALSO SAID TO BE GONE

FIGHT BEGAN SATURDAY

BETWEEN 2 AND 3 O'CLOCK IN
AFTERNOON, FOG LIFTED AND
TOGO FOUND HIS FOE

These ran in an extra printed at 5 A.M. Thus at breakfast New Yorkers read a story dated after lunch on the same day, Tokyo time. Because the *Times* story had flashed across the international date line en route to New York, *Times* readers had the then incredible experience of reading about news seemingly before it had even happened.

Though wireless had more than proved itself, years were to elapse before the full potentialities of the new tool were appreciated generally in the newspaper world. *The New York Times* hastened its development almost singlehandedly at first. Because Marconi had technical problems and difficulties in raising cash, regular wireless service had not been established immediately between Europe and America. It was not till 1907 that the *Times* could print this triumphant front-page story:

WIRELESS JOINS
TWO WORLDS

———

Marconi Transatlantic Service
Opened with a Dispatch to
The New York Times

In the same period, when aviation, too, was in its infancy, Ochs and Van Anda collaborated with boyish excitement in promoting news about the conquest of the air. The first story about Orville and Wilbur Wright's great exploit in leaving the ground in an airship had been sadly muffed; not till several days after the pioneer flight at Kitty Hawk, North Carolina, did the *Times* run this tiny piece:

AIRSHIP AFTER BUYER

———

Inventors of North Carolina Box Kite
Machine Want Government to
Purchase It

The inventors of the airship which is said to have made several successful flights in North Carolina near Kitty Hawk are anxious to sell the use of their device to the Government. They claim that they have solved the problem of aerial navigation and have never made a failure of any attempt to fly.

Their machine is an adaptation of the box-kite idea. The use to which the Government would put it would be in scouting and signal work and possibly in torpedo warfare.

After that, the *Times* paid closer attention to aviation. Competing in this department with the *World*, in 1908 the two papers tangled gloriously. The *World* had offered $10,000 prize to the first person to fly from Albany to New York City in a single day. When Glenn H. Curtiss took off from Albany on March 29, a *Times* reporter boarded a special train Van Anda had hired, and riding along the New York Central's regular tracks with a photographer beside him, kept up with Curtiss all along the route. Curtiss in his tiny biplane averaged 54 miles an hour on the flight, the *Times* train, 49.6 miles an hour; the two were never out of sight of each other along the 150-mile course. When Curtiss landed safely on the old Isham farm at Broadway and 214th Street, and got a hero's welcome, the *Times* already had the makings of a spectacular story—scooping the *World* on the happy outcome of the *World*'s own contest.

Relaxing his rule about keeping out of the limelight, Ochs himself offered a $10,000 prize later that same year for whoever would fly from New York to Philadelphia and back in a single day. Ochs had bought the Philadelphia *Public Ledger* recently, perhaps with the notion of eventually assembling a big chain of newspapers; however, he sold the *Public Ledger* at a profit, a year or so afterward, having decided that he could not devote enough attention to his New York newspaper, keep an eye on Chattanooga and put out a good daily in Philadelphia, too. The Philadelphia-New York air prize was one of the few joint projects of the *Times* and *Public Ledger*.

In this great age of exploration, Ochs almost by accident got the exclusive rights to Admiral Robert E. Peary's story of discovering the North Pole in 1909. For years, the doughty admiral had been equipping expeditions and trying in vain to reach the top of the world, and the *Herald* had helped finance several of these earlier attempts. In 1908 he had tried the *Herald* again, but the man he usually dealt with no longer worked there.

"He's over at the *Times* now," the admiral was told. And nobody else at the *Herald* was interested in buying the rights to a story that had failed to materialize several years in a row.

Admiral Peary was not a quitter. He walked up to the Times Tower, where William Reick, the former *Herald* man, introduced him to Adolph Ochs. After listening to the admiral, Ochs said crisply: "We will pay you four thousand dollars for the New York rights to your story." He also added that the *Times* would sell the Peary story to papers outside the city, but every cent of profit would go to the admiral himself.

Peary shook hands with the graying publisher and set about equipping his sixth polar expedition. Ochs was following all the plans gleefully when a sudden personal tragedy struck him a numbing blow. His beloved mother had come up from Chattanooga for a visit with him and Effie, and she had been having a fine time bustling about their house, coaxing nourishing food into her darling grandchild. But on January 31, 1908, her sturdy heart gave out.

Bertha Ochs was in her seventy-fifth year when she died, and Adolph was nearing his own fiftieth birthday. The shock of the loss stunned him for days. No son could have honored his mother more, nor striven harder to make her proud. She had lived to see him become one of the most respected men in the country, and his devotion to her had never wavered. Now this devotion made her death a cruel parting.

In silent grief, Ochs journeyed down to Chattanooga with her body and stood on a cold, bare hillside overlooking the city while she was buried. In keeping with her own staunch southern loyalty, the Chattanooga chapter of the Daughters of the Confederacy took part in the funeral ceremony, and a Confederate flag was draped over the coffin. Although his parents had lived together happily for so many years, their sad-comic political disagreement thus followed them both to their graves.

Back in New York, Ochs slowly regained his zest in hard work. But as the months went by, he began to await word from Admiral Peary with boyish excitement. The admiral had sailed north but was yet to be heard from—and Ochs himself was on vacation out west—when one evening a boy rushed into the *Times* newsroom waving a copy of the New York *Herald*.

"NORTH POLE REACHED!" the *Herald* trumpeted. Reached by whom? Not by Admiral Peary, but by a previously unknown Dr. Frederick A. Cook of Brooklyn. "After a prolonged fight with famine and frost, we at last succeeded in reaching the North Pole," Dr. Cook had wired the *Herald* from a north Canadian outpost he had just reached en route home. Only a few Eskimos had been with him, but he swore he had found the elusive pole. He had been paid $25,000 by the *Herald* for his exclusive story, it developed, and for once Van Anda had to swallow his pride and run a big spread on someone else's journalistic coup. The *Times* gave three pages to North Pole features, but it was careful to point out that independent proof of Cook's success was yet to be forthcoming. Ochs, by wire from his vacation hotel, fully endorsed Van Anda's caution.

They both had reason to be glad of this cautious care, for soon explorer circles on both sides of the Atlantic began to doubt Cook's word. He had no written records, no detailed scientific observations, Cook at last admitted. Soon he was being openly branded as a faker.

Then, at the height of the Cook controversy, the *Times* got a flash from Admiral Peary.

"I HAVE THE POLE!" Peary wired. "EXPECT TO ARRIVE CHATEAU BAY SEPTEMBER 7. SECURE CONTROL WIRE FOR ME THERE, AND ARRANGE TRANSMISSION BIG STORY."

So Ochs had been right in putting his trust in the grizzled admiral. Rushing back to the *Times* from his vacation, the publisher was on hand for the arrival of Peary's full account, which the *Times* splashed all over its front page. Ochs wrote to Effie, who had stayed behind:

> I find all well and the office in the greatest excitement about our marvelous and overwhelming good luck in regard to the Peary story. We are the exclusive publishers of Peary's story, and only through us can newspapers get the right to print it. Every newspaper in New York is in a panic about our tremendous scoop, and they are moving heaven and earth and offering all kinds of money to us and to our employees to get hold of it. Nothing in

American journalism equals this achievement of *The New York Times*.

> We are flooded with telegrams from newspapers all over the world asking to buy the story. Our orders exceed ten thousand dollars, all of which we shall give Peary. There is little doubt now that Cook is a faker.

Then sliding swiftly from publisher to husband, Ochs added: "Write me at once what you wish done in painting and papering the house."

While accident and his own good judgment had led Ochs to stake Peary to one more chance, the use the *Times* made of Peary's story could not be credited to luck. Every jot of scientific background data possible was incorporated in four days of spectacular layouts based on Peary's wires. For this Ochs—and Van Anda—deserved the applause they got in newspaper circles everywhere.

For months the great North Pole excitement did not die down. Cook held on to his claims at first, then later faded into the shadows as scientists the world over acclaimed Peary as the real discoverer of the pole. Before Cook finally disappeared from the newspapers, he had been indicted for mail fraud in another matter and eventually went to prison, while Peary and *The New York Times* went on to further triumphs.

Among newspapermen and the general public, the *Times* earned even greater applause a few years later with its stunning coverage of the great *Titanic* disaster.

On Sunday, April 14, 1912, the *Times* printed a two-column picture of the new luxury liner, the *Titanic*, the largest and most splendid ship ever launched. Steaming across the Atlantic on its maiden voyage, it was carrying 2,180 passengers and a large crew. A gala harbor welcome was being planned for its scheduled arrival on Tuesday morning.

As usual, on that Sunday Van Anda had come into the newsroom during the afternoon to see what stories were shaping up for the next morning's paper. He marked for the front page a routine political piece from Washington, a Brooklyn murder story and a suburban correspondent's piece about how the roof had fallen in that morning during a church service, killing two worshippers. As usual, Van Anda then went home for dinner and a nap, and toward midnight returned to shepherd an entirely routine issue of the paper through the composing room and press room.

At 1:20 A.M, on Monday morning, a copy boy handed Van Anda an AP bulletin:

CAPE RACE, NEWFOUNDLAND, SUNDAY NIGHT, APRIL 14—AT 10:25 O'CLOCK TONIGHT THE WHITE STAR LINE STEAMSHIP TITANIC CALLED "SOS" TO THE MARCONI STATION HERE, AND REPORTED HAVING STRUCK AN ICEBERG. THE STEAMER SAID IMMEDIATE ASSISTANCE WAS REQUIRED.

Van Anda picked up a telephone and ordered the presses stopped. He lit one of his big black cigars, then began showering assignments on the handful of sleepy reporters who were still hanging around. He summoned men back to work with terse phone calls. Ochs had let the managing editor hire the largest news staff in the city, and now at a moment of tingling journalistic challenge Van Anda showed he knew how to use his superb news-gathering machine.

He sent men to the clipping file to whip together a story about other ships that had hit icebergs in past years. He assigned men to rouse steamship officials sleeping in their homes in the far corners of the city and secure any possible shred of news from them. He had someone dig out the passenger list the White Star Line had sent into the office the preceding week, proudly listing all the eminent men and women booked for the *Titanic*'s maiden voyage. These included Mr. and Mrs. John Jacob Astor, Alfred G. Vanderbilt, Mr. and Mrs. Harry Widener.

But how did Van Anda know the *Titanic* was gone? The only hard news he had was the brief, inconclusive AP bulletin and a few more with only the scantiest details. But the editor had an encyclopedic general knowledge and the mind of a mathematician. Before starting his newspaper career, he had planned to make mathematics his life's work. With his cool, analytical mathematical mind and his vast store of background facts about ocean voyaging, he deduced that the great "unsinkable" ship was surely sinking.

While editors of other morning newspapers hedged with short, cautious, "it-is-rumored" stories, Van Anda plunged on a three-column front-page headline:

NEW LINER TITANIC HITS AN ICEBERG;

SINKING BY THE BOW AT MIDNIGHT;

WOMEN PUT OFF IN LIFEBOATS;

LAST WIRELESS AT 12:27 A.M. BLURRED

Coming into the newsroom the next morning, Ochs found his managing editor, red-eyed, still hunched over his desk planning the day's coverage of the *Titanic* story. Despite utter silence from the great ship, White Star officials were still refusing to confirm Van Anda's deduction. But he went ahead with feverish calls to correspondents in Montreal and Halifax, closer to the scene of possible rescue operations. While Ochs stood by, awed, Van Anda threw the whole majestic, news-gathering might of *The New York Times* into digging out the tragic truth. The entire front page of the next day's issue of the newspaper was devoted to telling the world about the Titanic disaster.

TITANIC SINKS FOUR HOURS AFTER HITTING ICEBERG;
866 RESCUED BY CARPATHIA, PROBABLY 1,250 PERISH;
ISMAY SAFE, MRS. ASTOR MAYBE, NOTED NAMES MISSING

This ran as a streamer headline across the entire front page, above a six-column-wide picture of the lost ship as she had sailed proudly out of Belfast harbor on her way to New York.

Then, on Thursday, when the *Carpathia* steamed into New York, every last man on the *Times* news staff, except for a handful watching over court and police beats, was sent out to interview *Titanic* survivors.

"I'm sending sixteen of you down to the pier, even though we have only these four passes," Arthur Greaves, the day city editor said, as Ochs and Van Anda listened approvingly. "Men without passes will have to try to get through to survivors—crew and passengers—on their police cards. If that can't be done, they will work as close in as they can and get survivors leaving the pier in cabs."

Other reporters were assigned to fan out around the city to see survivors at hotels. Cars and chauffeurs were hired to speed them to and from the office. Still other men were sent to meet the *Carpathia* on tugs, and to check on police arrangements for handling expected crowds at the pier. "The *Times* doesn't cover a story, it blankets it," reporters from other newspapers grumbled.

To the four men who had coveted pier cards—only four were given to each paper in the city—Greaves had these instructions: "I'm counting on you for the main survivor stories. Get all you can. Get Captain Rostrom of the *Carpathia*. Get Bruce Ismay of White Star. Get every possible member of the *Titanic* crew, especially the four officers who were saved. We must get the *Titanic* wireless man's story, if he's alive, and we want the *Carpathia*'s wireless man."

Like a general watching his troops march out to battle, Ochs stood and listened, occasionally offering a quiet suggestion. But he had full confidence in his captains and lieutenants and in every soldier on his staff. And they came through with flying colors.

Fifteen of the *Times*'s twenty-four pages on Friday were given over to *Titanic* stories. The streamer headline on page one said:

745 SAW TITANIC SINK WITH 1,595, HER BAND PLAYING;
HIT ICEBERG AT 21 KNOTS, AND TORE HER BOTTOM OUT;
"I'LL FOLLOW THE SHIP," LAST WORDS OF CAPTAIN SMITH.
MANY WOMEN STAYED TO PERISH WITH THEIR HUSBANDS

The lead story started:

In a clear, starlit night that showed a clear deep blue sea for miles and miles, the *Titanic*, an hour after she had struck a submerged iceberg at full speed, head-on, sank slowly to her ocean grave.

Her band, lined on board, was playing pleasant music as she sank in full view of her wretched survivors. And those left of her passengers and crew—fully two-thirds—stood quietly resigned on deck, awaiting the final plunge . . . .

Reading that issue of *The New York Times*, editors on other papers could only shrug and murmur that if they had had the same resources at their disposal, they might have been able to make a better showing. But faced with a journalistic feat so far above compare, they could be generous, too. Ochs had himself a real newspaper, they told each other, a newspaperman's newspaper.

Foreign publishers were equally generous. Cables of praise for the fabulous *Titanic* coverage showered on Ochs from Rome, Paris and London. Several years later, visiting in London and calling on Lord Northcliffe, editor of London's *Daily Mail*, Ochs watched Northcliffe open a drawer in his desk and take out *The New York Times* of Friday, April 19, 1912, the Friday when the *Titanic* survivors' stories had run. "We keep this," Lord Northcliffe said, "as an example of the greatest accomplishment in news reporting."

13

If Ochs had shown great good judgment in many matters, in one at least he failed to take a sufficiently bold line. By 1912, after only seven years in the grandiose Times Tower, *The New York Times* was already sorely cramped for space. The building was tall, but it was narrow, of necessity, because of the limited land that had been available. Not even Ochs had foreseen how fast his newspaper would keep expanding.

Ochs was satisfied to have built one spectacular New York monument, so when it came time to build again, he aimed merely for convenience. In 1913, the men and machines that put out *The New York Times* moved a block away, to a big, square new plant on West Forty-third Street. To the public, the Times Tower was still the newspaper's home, and for many years the ribbon of electric-light news bulletins and a ground floor classified ad office kept this impression alive. But from 1913 on, the *Times* was produced in the new Times Annex, although the newspaper did not sell the Times Tower till 1960.

In the calmer, comparatively serene days before the first World War, when there was no radio or television and when the prediction seemed outlandish that someday a person could pick up a telephone in his own house and call a friend in London, Ochs already had upsetting forebodings. It was marvelous that miracles of communication were making the world shrink, but it was terrifying, too. He saw that quarrels flaring up in the Old World were bound to involve the New World as well, for the United States had become a most powerful nation. Ochs had watched the process with his own keen blue eyes, and he knew, from firsthand observation, that the change had not gone unnoticed on the other side of the Atlantic.

A regular visitor abroad, he took time out for light-hearted pleasure. But he also made it a point to meet with foreign publishers and his own foreign reporters. He was entertained by prominent diplomats everywhere, and he was sufficiently perceptive to be aware of the inevitable involvement of the United States in any major clash between the opposing powers then building up in Europe.

As early as 1908, the *Times* had sent a man to interview Kaiser Wilhelm II of Germany, and the blustery Emperor had talked such shocking war talk that the reporter cabled home for guidance before sending his story.

For two hours, the Kaiser had ranted against Britain's "ninny" rulers and the Roman Catholic Church and the "yellow menace" of Japan. To ensure the future of the world, he said flatly, he expected to fight England soon.

"The Bible is full of good fighting—jolly good fights," Kaiser Wilhelm said. "It is a mistaken idea that Christianity has no countenance for war."

When a guarded summary of all this reached the *Times* in New York, it was carried directly to Ochs's desk. Ochs called in his top editors, and they agreed to have William B. Hale, the man who had talked with the Kaiser, come home to tell his tale in person. A thoroughly reliable reporter, who had trained for the ministry before switching to journalism, Hale could be trusted, but if what he was hinting was to be published it could easily be the spark that touched off open war between Germany and Great Britain.

Hale came home, and his notes proved even more fiery than his cabled summary had hinted. Ochs hated the thought of suppressing a story, any legitimate news story; his whole publishing career had been founded on the cornerstone of printing all the news.

"But I don't think we should print this," he told his editors. Citizen first and publisher second, he brought Hale down to Washington to read his notes to President Theodore Roosevelt.

"Astonishing stuff," Roosevelt said. "I don't believe the Emperor wanted this stuff published. If he did, he's a goose. Yet I know he's very impulsive."

As President of the United States in peacetime, Roosevelt told Ochs, he did not have the authority to ask that the story be killed. But, he added, he thought the *Times* would save the world great agony if it killed the story. Ochs nodded. Back in New York, he locked Hale's notes in his own private safe.

But the mounting tension in Europe did not subside. In the summer of 1914, Archduke Francis Ferdinand, heir to the Austrian throne, was shot and killed in Sarajevo by a Serbian terrorist. Germany joined Austria in demanding drastic measures by Serbia to stop anti-Austrian intrigue there, and the great powers of England and France joined Russia in backing Serbia's refusal. In August, war came.

Ochs threw the unparalleled resources of *The New York Times* into covering the great conflict. Late in August, before even the State Department in Washington had seen the documents involved, the *Times* printed—on six full pages—"The Complete Correspondence That Led Up To England's Declaration of War Against Germany." This famed British White Paper, containing copies of 159 notes exchanged between Britain and Germany, gave every reader the materials with which to draw his own conclusions about the rights and wrongs of Britain's case. Then the following day, Germany's version of the same correspondence was published, without so much as a comma changed from the material provided by the Kaiser's foreign office.

No other newspaper had the staff or the cash to indulge in such spectacular efforts. Printing all these tens of thousands of words took more manpower and money than any other newspaper, foreign or domestic, could afford. True, other newspapers had larger circulations and some few even had larger advertising revenue, but no other publisher was operating on Ochs's philosophy: plow back every penny of profit, if necessary, to pay for printing all the news.

From his early days on *The New York Times*, Ochs believed the reader was entitled to every pertinent piece of information on a public question, in order to form his own judgment. As soon as he could afford it, he began printing the complete text of every major address by important political leaders, regardless of party. The text of a city budget or proposed new law on a controversial issue also was printed.

"But who wants to read all those words?" some of his editors asked at first.

But Ochs knew what he was about, and soon libraries throughout the land, other newspaper offices, anybody requiring full information on a current issue consulted *The New York Times*. For students and research workers, the *Times* was invaluable. As much as any other single ingredient, this insistence by Ochs on printing "dull" texts ensured the pre-eminence of his newspaper.

Even during the early years of the first World War, before this nation became directly involved, he spent a small fortune on cable and wireless charges, on salaries, on paper and ink to print the most complete possible war news coverage. Texts of official communiqués appeared as issued by the headquarters of both sides. As far as humanly possible, equal play was given in the *Times* news columns to German and British claims.

But editorially, on the page devoted to opinion, the *Times* leaned more and more toward the British cause, just as much as America was beginning to do, too. "The *Times* is in the pay of the British," was muttered angrily in pro-German circles. Rumors that Ochs was a puppet of the British government began circulating. The rumor even reached Congress, and in the highly emotional climate developing as the United States inched closer to participation in the war, the editor of *The New York Times* was subpoenaed to answer questions before a Senate committee. Charles Miller, still the august chief of the *Times* editorial page, was asked:

"Has the *Times* any business connections of any character in England?"

"None whatever," Miller said firmly, "except that we maintain an office there and have our own employees there, our correspondents. There is no business connection with anybody in England."

Miller also answered a long series of questions clearly designed to find out whether Adolph Ochs did truly have complete control of *The New York Times*. In the *Times* the next morning, there appeared an editorial saying:

> That there may be no cause to believe that Mr. Miller's answer to the impertinent inquiry about Mr. Ochs's private affairs does not fully and satisfactorily end the inquiry, Mr. Ochs wishes to make the assertion as broad and as sweeping as language will permit that he is in possession, free and unencumbered, of the controlling and majority interest of the stock of the New York Times Company, and has no associate in that possession, and is not beholden or accountable to any person or interest in England or anywhere else in the world, nor has he ever been beholden or accountable in any form, shape or fashion, financial or otherwise, for the conduct of *The New York Times*, except to his own conscience and to the respect and confidence of the newspaper-reading public, and particularly to the readers of *The New York Times*—and more particularly to the respect and confidence of those who are associated with him in producing *The New York Times* and expressing its opinions.

That Ochs did have, in full measure, the respect and confidence of his staff was proved in 1916 on the twentieth anniversary of his assuming control of the newspaper. A thick leather album more than two feet square was presented to him then, with a flowery message of appreciation inscribed on its opening page. It was hand-lettered in gold and crimson, very much in the manner of a medieval, illuminated manuscript.

Then, more down to earth, came page after page of personal letters penned by his *New York Times* associates, and in the sentences of these less elaborate missives the thread of devotion was clearly apparent. At the back of the album were these mundane but not irrelevant figures: average daily circulation of *The New York Times* in 1916, 344,631; advertising lineage, 10,832,365 lines.

As 1916 gave way to 1917 there was no longer any argument about whether the pro-Allied stand taken by the *Times* and by most other New York newspapers, too, was unpatriotic. Germany's declaration of unrestricted submarine war brought American sentiment firmly to the Allied side, and in April President Woodrow Wilson asked Congress to join the Allies' fight against Germany.

The entry of the United States into the war brought one personal crisis to Adolph Ochs. His daughter, Iphigene, pretty and dark-eyed at twenty-five, met a handsome young man while vacationing at their summer home on Lake George. She had known him casually when she attended Barnard and he Columbia but now his attractiveness was enhanced by the uniform he was wearing. With her cousin, Julius Ochs Adler, he was training for overseas duty at an Army camp near the upstate New York lake. Toward autumn, Iffy confounded her father by telling him she wanted to marry this Lieutenant Arthur Hays Sulzberger.

"What do you want to get married for?" the startled father sputtered. "You have a good home. What's the sense of it?"

Ochs had nothing against the young man, nor marriage for that matter, but it never occurred to him that she could be interested in anyone not in the newspaper business. Sulzberger's family, an old and respected Jewish family with forebears going back to the Revolutionary War, were cotton merchants, and Arthur had expected to join the family business when the war intervened.

But Iffy was her father's daughter. When she had her heart set on something, she generally found a way to get it. Her heart was set on marrying the handsome lieutenant, and his on marrying her, so between them, they hatched a simple plot.

"Father doesn't dislike you," Iffy assured her young man. "But he's worried about the newspaper. He's never said it in so many words, but I'm sure—even if he wouldn't hear of my working at the *Times* myself—that he'd like me to marry a newspaperman. He can't bear thinking the *Times* won't always be run the way he runs it. He'd feel safer if it stayed in the family. Couldn't you promise him you'd work there after the war?"

"But what could I do there?" Lieutenant Sulzberger had never seen the inside of a newspaper office.

"You'll learn," Iffy said firmly. And the lieutenant was willing. He spoke up on the subject to his prospective father-in-law, and the simple plot succeeded. Too much the doting parent to thwart his daughter on a matter like this, the fifty-nine-year-old publisher gave his consent to the marriage, although he was still not quite convinced that his son-in-law could make any important contribution to *The New York Times*. On November 17, 1917, Iphigene Ochs became Iphigene Sulzberger at an elegant wedding in the Ochs home on West Seventy-fifth Street.

While Iffy followed her husband to an artillery camp in Ohio, the tempo of the war overseas quickened. As American troops marched into battle "over there," *The New York Times* printed war news at the cost of $15,000 a week in cable charges alone—more than Henry Raymond had spent on foreign news in a whole year.

But don't worry about the money, Ochs told his editors. He wanted complete coverage and money was no object. In fact he was leaving out sixty to seventy columns of advertising every day, since he had neither the paper nor the press capacity to print all the news streaming in, plus all the advertising being offered the *Times*.

The Allied armies continued to advance during the spring and summer, and with the approach of autumn, Germany's partner, Austria, began to collapse. This triumph for the Allied cause, by an incredible series of coincidences, plunged Adolph Ochs and his *New York Times* into the worst storm either had ever had to weather.

On a Sunday in September, the spectacular news flashed into Forty-third Street that Austria was suing for peace. Ochs had gone up to his summer home in Lake George for the weekend, and when Van Anda read the flash, unaccountably he did not call the publisher. He called Charles Miller, the chief editorial writer, at home in Great Neck on Long Island, and told him excitedly: "This is the beginning of the end!" Miller, staid and cautious during all of his thirty-four years as head of the *Times* editorial page, unaccountably did not call Ochs before dashing off an editorial at home.

He wrote jubilantly:

> Reason and humanity demand that the Austrian invitation be accepted. The case for a conference is presented with extraordinary eloquence and force. . . . We cannot imagine that the invitation will be declined. . . .When we consider the deluge of blood that has been poured out in this war, the

incalculable waste of treasure, the ruin it has wrought, the grief that wrings millions of hearts because of it, we must conclude that only madness or the soulless depravity of someone of the belligerent powers could obstruct or defeat the purpose of the conference.

Miller read this over the telephone to a reporter who took down every tingling word. Then Van Anda read it, nodded, and let it go through.

When it appeared in *The New York Times* of September 16, 1918, a huge, angry wave burst upon the respected newspaper. Furious telephone calls and wires and cables flooded the office. Other newspapers printed fierce editorials denouncing the *Times* for "running up the white flag." At a time when it was patriotic to wear a lapel button that said "U.S. Club"—meaning "Unconditional Surrender Club"—even to suggest negotiating with the enemy was almost treason. The policy of the United States government and its Allies was to seek the unconditional surrender of its enemies, not a negotiated peace. Miller's hasty words almost killed the *Times* and Adolph Ochs.

How had the editor's judgment slipped so disastrously? Maybe if he had been in the office, and read proof of what he had written, he might have modified his tone, or called Ochs up in Lake George before sending the piece to the composing room.

But why didn't Van Anda catch the offending editorial in time? The only answer both men could give was that, under pressure, they unaccountably erred.

The storm it aroused was unbelievable. The Union League Club of New York, composed of many of the city's most eminent men, met to censure the *Times*. From London and Paris, irate messages poured down on Ochs. From Washington, it was reported that President Wilson was furious with the publisher. Hurrying back from Lake George, Ochs found more than 3,000 bitter telegrams.

So shaken he could hardly speak, Ochs sat dazed at his desk wondering if all his long years of work were now to end with disgrace. Why were people so unreasonable? Must one mistake outweigh so many more worthy actions? Surely even *The New York Times* was entitled to one lapse, yet all this mail piling up about him held hardly a hint of charity. At the open door of his office, assistants huddled, wondering whether to summon a doctor.

But although Ochs sat for hours without speaking, he did speak, slowly and without anger, to Miller and Van Anda. Let there be another editorial asserting the *Times*'s loyalty, he said, and full coverage of the war as usual. He did not storm at either man; he knew them too well to blame them for this single error.

Although Ochs had not been in the office when the peace editorial had been written, and although he had not even seen it before it appeared in print, he refused to say so publicly. As publisher, he had always stood by his staff, and he would do so now. To a friend who begged him to speak out, to temper the violence of the personal attacks being made on him, he said: "I could not do such a thing. I have always accepted public praise and public approval of the many great editorials Mr. Miller has written for the *Times*. When there is blame instead of praise I must share that, too."

Only to President Wilson did Ochs try to explain the true situation. He went down to Washington and spent several hours with Colonel Edward M. House, the President's chief adviser, telling him how the editorial happened, pleading for understanding in the White House. The *Times* had always been patriotic, Ochs said, sick at having to justify his newspaper at this late date.

Then sunk in melancholy, Ochs returned to New York and tried to go through the motions of attending to his publishing duties. But for the first time in his career, his heart was not in his work. Effie worried as he brooded day and night, heedless of all the little details that had always seemed so absorbing. His energy failed him, too, and doctors warned he was on the verge of nervous collapse.

Not even the joyous hysteria as the war ended in November brought him out of his gloom. With the coming of peace, the furor about the *Times* editorial was gradually forgotten by its readers, but its publisher remained a moody, silent shadow of his former self.

14

Very slowly Ochs emerged from his deep depression. As the months passed, he no longer told Effie he ought to quit and let a trustee take over the *Times*, in order to restore public confidence in the paper. Even he could see that the public's confidence was more than restored by one spectacular feat after another. In the immediate post-war years, the *Times* printed every word of the Versailles Treaty—eight full pages of type; it scooped every other paper on the east coast with complete coverage of the 1920 Democratic Convention in San Francisco; it pioneered in presenting long, accurate stories about science news like Einstein's theory of relativity, and the discovery in Egypt of the 3,000-year-old tomb of King Tut-ankh-Amen.

But much as Ochs rejoiced at seeing his newspaper on the high road again, it wasn't that which pulled him out of his blue mood. The cure started right in his own home. With the end of the war, Lieutenant Sulzberger left the Army and the young couple moved into the Ochs house on Seventy-fifth

Street. It was a big, gloomy house full of ornate statuary and overstuffed plush furniture. It was good to have cheery young voices in it again, and with the birth of his first grandchild, the house changed and Ochs changed. Suddenly he was like his old self again. "My angel!" he called baby Marian, and he never missed a night in the nursery and always with an armload of new toys. A man who adored children, he had lived much of his adult life with only one child on whom to lavish his overflowing love. Now, as a magnificent bonus, he had a new baby.

And the baby's father was proving a pleasant surprise, too. Ochs had quietly decided that his son-in-law was a nice enough young fellow, charming and polished, but he put little hope in Sulzberger's turning into a newspaperman. Let him make Iffy happy and that would be enough. So when Arthur appeared at the *Times* to make good his promise about learning the business, Ochs shunted him to a side office where he had practically nothing to do. "Give him some little jobs," he told an assistant.

Sulzberger thought he would like to try his hand at writing, but the only "little job" the puzzled assistant could think of for him was helping tabulate contributions to the *Times* Hundred Neediest Cases Fund. This was a yearly appeal Ochs had started after an experience that had troubled him. On a Christmas Day, after a hearty turkey dinner at home, he went for a walk from Seventy-fifth Street to Times Square. He strode along feeling well-fed and at peace with the world, when a shabby but neat man approached him.

"I've just had a good Christmas dinner at the YMCA," the man said, "but I wonder if you could help me to pay for a bed tonight. I have no money."

Ochs eyed him carefully and decided he looked respectable. He gave him a few dollars along with one of his cards. "If you're looking for a job," he said, "come in and see me tomorrow."

The man appeared the next morning, and Ochs found a job for him. He never told his wife and daughter the man's name; nobody at the *Times*, where the man worked for years, ever knew how Ochs had come to hire him. The incident set Ochs thinking about the deep inner satisfaction he himself had gotten from helping a man down on his luck. Maybe other people would be grateful for the opportunity of doing something for someone, particularly at the Christmas season. The following year he asked to have a reporter gather from the files of several private welfare agencies the stories of "New York's Hundred Neediest Cases," and these ran in the *Times* before the Christmas season. Response from readers was immediate; in fact, one very prosperous reader offered to give the *Times* $1,000,000 outright, to use every year to aid the needy, but Ochs turned down the gift. The *Times* was not primarily a charitable organization, he explained, and his purpose in printing the appeal for funds every year was to encourage its readers to remember the unfortunate anew, and to help them through established charities.

It was on this pet project of his that Arthur Sulzberger spent his first few months at the *Times*. He worked so diligently totaling checks and forwarding contributions to the charitable agencies that after Christmas his father-in-law gave him an assignment closer to the heart of newspapering. He told him to look into ways and means of increasing the *Times*'s supply of newsprint, the blank paper essential for printing news. In those days, the *Times* was running about forty-eight pages every day, a fat paper compared to most, but Ochs was not satisfied. He had the news and the advertising to fill more pages every day, if only he could get paper. Sulzberger did so well dickering with Canadian paper mills that Ochs began to eye his son-in-law with more respect.

"If you'd picked a husband just with my interests in mind," he told his daughter, "you couldn't have done better."

The young Sulzbergers presented him with another granddaughter in 1921, and now he had two angels, Marian and Ruth.

In the spring, the sixty-three-year-old publisher found a different and delightful kind of medicine to bring back still more of his old gusto. Early in May, he received a touching letter from Knoxville telling him that the Chamber of Commerce there was planning a party for Captain William Rule—the same Captain Rule young Muley Ochs had swept and polished for so many years earlier. Could the eminent New York publisher, Adolph S. Ochs, find time to come down to Tennessee to help celebrate Captain Rule's eighty-second birthday?

This was exactly the sort of sentimental pilgrimage to shake Ochs out of the last traces of his blue mood. From the instant he stepped off the train, his step took on a boyish briskness. At the station to meet him was walrus-moustached Henry Clay Collins, the kindly print shop foreman who had walked him home past the cemetery so many mornings years ago. The walrus moustache was snow-white now, for Collins was well past eighty, but for the moment neither man paid any mind to the half-century that had elapsed since they had worked together.

In the bustling station, Ochs had only to close his eyes and he could recall every foot of the route he used to follow, delivering *Chronicles* in the darkness when he had been a boy of eleven. Soon Ochs and Collins were strolling through the streets of Knoxville, retracing the old route street by street. At length, the two happy snow-thatched gentlemen turned in at the alley where the Knoxville *Chronicle* still was being printed, and walked into the old-fashioned office where Captain Rule himself sat hunched over his roll-top desk.

To the nostalgic Adolph Ochs, the scene seemed no different from his first view of it, except that over the old desk there were two portraits instead of the one he remembered in his youth. Alongside the Louisville *Courier-Journal*'s Henry Watterson, the idol of many southern newspapermen, there was a framed photograph of himself.

Captain Rule was bent and feeble now, but his guffawing laugh had the same old ring. He and Ochs and Collins sat for hours trading old-time memories, laughing together over them, and then the next day at the Chamber of Commerce party they reminisced some more. As the most eminent guest, Ochs was called upon to speak, but he kept the spotlight where it belonged—on the captain, not himself.

"Should I assist in any effort to make a lion of an Ochs," he said, "I fear I might display myself as an ass. I have come here tonight because I love Captain Rule. As an office boy, I trimmed the lamps in his office. I always tried to keep them bright and burning, and I'm glad to say that Captain Rule has kept them bright through all the years that have passed."

Even back in New York, the nostalgic happiness held. Ochs plunged into a series of projects planned to celebrate his twenty-fifth anniversary with *The New York Times*, among them a history of the newspaper, written by one of its top reporters, Elmer Davis, who later became a prominent radio commentator.

Ochs also worked on a summary of the newspaper's achievements, printed in the issue of August 18, 1921, describing its many journalistic firsts. But back of these lay one cold financial fact Ochs did not brag about—that of the $100,000,000 the paper had earned during his quarter-century at its helm, he had used less than four percent to pay dividends to stockholders. All the rest of the income had been spent on covering the news. As the *Times* earned more money, he spent more to expand his staff and improve his equipment. This, above anything else, was the key to Ochs's success. He was not greedy for money in his own pocket; what could have been clear profit, he put back into the paper.

Though Ochs was not a man to frown on sentimental ceremony, he had little taste for public applause. He never forgot that he had quit school at fifteen, and felt embarrassed when great universities showered honorary degrees on him. At one point, when he was asked to referee a Harvard-Yale debate, he declined, pleading business pressure, then wrote to one of his sisters: "I turned down the debate bid on the theory that the higher a monkey climbs the more he shows his tail."

This was the man Dr. Nicholas Murray Butler of Columbia University, in bestowing an honorary LL.D., called "the master mind of journalism in any land."

But Ochs did have his touch of vanity. Writing home from Europe, he told Effie: "Strangers say my face resembles that of G.W. I mean the Father of My Country. I am naturally quite flattered." And from then on, Ochs did his best to emphasize the resemblance, which was genuine, by brushing his thick white hair on both sides of his bald pate into something very similar to the powdered wig worn by George Washington.

Perhaps because of the stresses of the twenty-fifth anniversary celebration, Ochs worked too hard in the summer and fall of 1921. He stayed up late too many evenings; he ate too much rich food, and one morning late in the autumn he collapsed. His doctor prescribed a long rest, and read him a lecture about the pace suitable for a man of his age. With Effie and a party of old friends, he left for a leisurely Mediterranean cruise. But he was too much of a celebrity now to enjoy a carefree vacation. At Gibraltar, the British governor greeted him with ceremony; in Rome, he put on white tie and tails for an audience with the Pope; in Cairo, he saw the Sultan; in Constantinople and Jerusalem he was taken on long, tiring ceremonial inspection side trips, like visiting royalty. When they got to Paris he had to stay in bed, and after a few days of no banquets and no split-second schedule he felt better, and returned to New York quite refreshed. But never again would he be able to call on a limitless supply of energy. He was not a sick man, but he wasn't well, either.

Although he continued to keep his finger on every phase of *Times* operation, more and more he did this away from the paper. Reading the *Times* in his library at home, if he found an error in the one-line headline of a one-paragraph story at the bottom of page thirty-seven, he would pick up the telephone and call the paper. Edwin L. James, who succeeded Van Anda as managing editor, said: "He would usually begin, not with a complaint but with a compliment on the handling of some important story on the front page, and, of course, I would be elated. Then he would add, as if it were an afterthought, 'By the way, there is a head on page thirty-seven that I think is hardly adequate.' I would look at it, and it would be awful. But the previous compliment would have cushioned the shock so that I wouldn't be downcast, merely determined not to let it happen again."

In these months, Ochs also assigned an increasing load of responsibility to his son-in-law, Arthur Sulzberger. From the sub-basement pressroom to the executive suites on the fourteenth floor, the former lieutenant was gradually absorbing newspaper know-how. Now that he had proved himself an apt pupil, he was getting a chance to tackle all sorts of problems, for even without any words being spoken on the subject, it was growing clear that someday he would become master of the whole domain.

On doctor's orders, Ochs now took frequent vacations and he spent happy hours just playing with his grandchildren. His third granddaughter, Judith, was born in 1923; and three years later came Arthur Ochs Sulzberger, named both for his father and grandfather.

If Granddaddy Ochs did not thoroughly spoil his four grandchildren, it was not for want of trying. He could not come home without a sack of parcels for them, and finally their father put his foot down. "Tell your father," he told Iffy. "No more presents for the children, or I'll have to do something about it." Whether Iffy relayed the message or not, the nightly Santa Claus performance kept right on, so Sulzberger did something about it. He, too, came home loaded down with dolls and games and trucks. For a glorious week or so, the children lived in a wonderland of new toys till the grown-ups in the family had a good laugh and the flood of presents stopped.

From then on, Granddaddy tried hard not to spoil the youngsters, but when birthdays came he was incorrigible. Not only did he think of marvelous presents, but he also managed to arrive home at the proper moment at every birthday party, when all the boys and girls were sitting properly at the table eating their cake in a most mannerly way under Effie's and Iffy's approving eyes. Then he swept in with a bag of tin whistles or toy drums, anything capable of creating ear-splitting din. "Let's see who can make the most noise," Granddaddy said cheerfully. "Come on, let's have a good, loud parade." And as the women watched, helpless, a magnificently noisy parade got organized.

Summers were idyllic for the four youngsters. Often with a whole raft of cousins, they spent the warm months up at Lake George, singing, splashing and having a generally glorious time. Their grandparents bought them a pony and built them a playhouse, and if their parents went off on a trip to Europe alone, the children were far from neglected.

Granddaddy delighted in appearing while the children were eating, and sat with them, nibbling a taste from every plate. Even at Lake George, a certain formality was preserved, and the grown-ups dined alone usually, but Ochs did have some wonderfully original ideas about what was suitable for children.

Amid all the hilarity, there were a few solemn moments at Lake George. One of them came with stunning suddenness when Ochs was being shaved one morning by Jules, his French valet, who had been working for him for more than twenty years. A little man who walked on his toes, Jules was the great good friend of the children as well as the valued confidante of his employer.

Without any warning, he had a heart attack that morning and died.

Ochs, knowing that Jules was a Catholic, gravely got in touch with the local parish to arrange for a Catholic funeral. But the priest objected, saying that in all his years at Lake George, Jules had never come to church there. In France, Ochs had met Jules's mother, and he knew the old lady would be heartsick if her son were buried out of the family's faith, so he telephoned his friend Cardinal Gibbon in New York. The Cardinal heard him out about the parish priest's objections, then said: "How does he know he didn't go to church in New York?" After much telephoning, a funeral service in nearby Glens Falls was arranged, with the burial to be in New York City. All the way down in the train, Ochs read quietly to himself from a Jewish prayer book he had brought along with him. Then at the cemetery, as the coffin was lowered he stepped forward and read aloud from a section he had marked in his book, the prayer for the dead.

To Ochs, religion was a private affair, not to be paraded in public. Brought up in a devout Jewish household, he believed in the faith of his fathers, and though he associated with men of all faiths he never forsook his own. In 1926, he gave $400,000 to the congregation in Chattanooga where his family had worshipped, for the construction of a new temple and community center as a memorial to his parents.

This was only one of his many benefactions, most of them given quietly or even anonymously. "To ask for gratitude is to ask to be repaid twice," he once told his daughter. "The person who gives has the fun of giving." And when a grateful recipient tried to thank him, he said: "Don't thank me. Just congratulate me that I'm in a position to be able to do it."

There is no record of the twenty-dollar bills Ochs pressed on an old friend with a sick wife or on a *Times* porter with a sick child. There is a record, though, that he gave $532,000 to the American Council of Learned Societies to help it produce its masterly *Dictionary of American Biography* and that he gave $200,000 to Princeton University Library to pay for compiling *The Papers of Thomas Jefferson.*

Much of Ochs's private philanthropy was given in New York—and among the recipients of his generosity, besides the temple where he worshipped, was the Episcopal Cathedral of St. John the Divine, to which he contributed $10,000 and a pair of gold candlesticks because he felt that any citizen, regardless of his religion, should be honored to help build this beautiful cathedral for the city. However, much of his philanthropy went to Chattanooga.

Back in the 1880's, when the bitterness of the Civil War was only beginning to disappear, he had been chairman of the Chickamauga Memorial Association, a group formed to plan for a national park on the site of the great Civil War battlefield. In 1889, in a huge, flag-draped tent at a stirring rally, he had presided over the first joint meeting of veterans from the Confederate forces and from the Union Army, now working together on this peaceful project.

All through his busy years in New York, Ochs kept in touch with Chattanooga friends working on the national park project. As early as 1890, President Benjamin Harrison had signed an act establishing the Chickamauga and Chattanooga National Military Park, the first such in the country. However, the glorious summit of Lookout Mountain, where the Battle Above the Clouds had been fought, was not included because much of the land was privately owned by promoters of a tourist resort scheme. In the 1920's, Ochs and his old friends finally got title to 2,700 acres on the slopes of the mountain, and deeded this to the nation; Ochs himself invested $150,000 in rebuilding the old road up to the summit.

So in 1928 the city of Chattanooga decided to thank its native, and whether he wanted to be thanked or not, Adolph Ochs got one of the most elaborate thank-yous in three emotion-packed days late in June of that year.

Really it was a triple celebration. Three months earlier, in March, Ochs had reached the milestone of his seventieth birthday, an occasion marked by hundreds of congratulatory messages. "Please accept my hearty good wishes on your birthday anniversary," President Calvin Coolidge wired from the White House. "Newspapermen all over the world will today reflect with pride and admiration on your distinguished career . . . you are an inspiration to us all," Viscount Rothermere cabled from London.

Now, to celebrate this seventieth birthday—and the fiftieth anniversary of the day a callow boy took over the Chattanooga *Times* with a borrowed $250—the city of Chattanooga paid its homage to Adolph Ochs.

An American Legion band met the special train on which Ochs, Effie and about sixty New York friends arrived on the evening of June 29. There was a parade to the new Lookout Mountain Hotel, lit by flashing beams from the top of the Chattanooga Savings Bank Building. The next two days, there were luncheons, a boat ride, a military review, a seven-course banquet. Then there was a ceremony at which the mayor handed Ochs a gold key to the city, along with a scroll designating him "Citizen Emeritus of Chattanooga."

To celebrate the third happy occasion—the completion of the dreamed-of national park project—a ceremony was held on the mountainside and the new road to the summit was formally named Ochs Highway. Plans for a museum at the summit were disclosed then, and the museum, too, would be named for him.

"What greater glory can come to a man, what more beautiful crown than the love and affection of neighbors?" Ochs said with tears in his eyes.

Then there was another dinner, this one attended by old friends brought over from Knoxville on a special bus. Among them were Captain Rule and Henry Clay Collins, who sat smiling proudly at the head table through the long succession of congratulatory speeches and messages.

Later, home in Knoxville, Captain Rule wrote an editorial about the great occasion, one of the last editorials he was to write.

> One of the number present was the humble writer, who enjoys the distinction of having employed Mr. Ochs, then a mere lad, in a newspaper office, and has, as a matter of course, kept an eye upon him, and seen him become the most prosperous newspaper publisher in the whole world. His old friends remain his friends. Friendship is not weakened by the lapse of time. *His* friendship has not, and when counsel is sought he gives it and its soundness ungrudgingly. . . .
>
> What is said here, is said without his knowledge or consent. It is a case of "out of the abundance of the heart, the mouth (or pen) speaketh."

One month later, Captain Rule died.

15

During the next few years Ochs was forced to give up more and more of his activities. He had no acute illness, the doctors told Effie, but his sturdy heart was running out of energy. He continued as unquestioned chief of *The New York Times*, the one man responsible for major decisions, but he no longer strode briskly through his domain offering a suggestion here, a willing ear there.

Now he relied more and more on his son-in-law. Every evening, Arthur would bring him firsthand accounts of the day's happenings, and they would talk over impending problems together. Ochs also kept in touch with other top aides by telephone, and they would often come up to Seventy-fifth Street after work for a leisurely conference in the big oak-paneled library on the second floor. Despite the lessening of his tasks, Ochs continued to grow more frail. His once bouncy spirits gave way more and more to moods of gloomy silence.

In 1930, his doctors prescribed a calmer atmosphere than that of New York City, so the house on Seventy-fifth Street was sold after so many years and the family moved to a great, rambling house in White Plains. This was only twenty miles north of the city but it had open country and placid woods and meadows. His new home was like the estate of an English squire, with tennis courts and a private lake. Ochs named it Hillandale.

In this peaceful retreat, Ochs had a large, pleasant attic room fitted out as an office, where he spent a few hours every day keeping in touch with New York by telephone. He also had a gracious, oak-paneled library like the one in his city home, and many evenings he sat there after dinner conferring with one or another of his executives about plans for the *Times*—to buy stock in a Canadian paper mill; to expand Washington coverage; to add new features to the Sunday paper, then selling almost 750,000 copies every week, although the daily circulation still hovered under the 500,000 mark. One feature Ochs would not add was a comics section, nor did he look kindly on suggestions for cake-baking recipes or child care hints. Much as he liked the ladies, he saw no need for a women's page in a serious newspaper, and he even frowned on hiring women reporters, feeling that they, too, were out of place at the *Times*. Apart from these prejudices, Ochs listened willingly to suggestions from his editors.

Unlike many other successful newspaper publishers, especially Joseph Pulitzer, Ochs had never insisted on making every trivial decision himself. He had never peppered his aides with sharp instructions about how to play every story, even when he was spending six days a week at the *Times*. So now he had a confident, competent team to carry on in his absence.

In these ever lonelier months up in White Plains, Ochs had ample time to reflect on the future of his newspaper, and to ponder a new lesson involving the long-dead Pulitzer. Pulitzer, too, had believed his own newspaper was more than just a profitable private business, that it was a public service, an institution of great importance in a democracy; and after his early, screaming-headline fight with Hearst, he had transformed the *World* into a responsible and still lively paper that truly performed outstanding journalistic service. Even when shattered nerves kept him from directing the paper in person, Pulitzer had kept his finger on every phase of the *World*'s operation, dictating reams of memos every day from his sound-proofed yacht, and the *World* had prospered. It was one of the most readable, intelligently edited newspapers ever to appear in New York or any other city, and it won wide acclaim as the leader of the liberal wing of the Democratic party, just as *The New York Times* was generally regarded as the spokesman for the party's conservative wing. But with his reams of memos, Pulitzer had failed to build up independent judgment among his top men, and when the publisher died in 1911 he left no experienced successor.

On momentum, the paper continued to come out for another twenty years, and these were golden years in its history. Some say New York has never had a newspaper the equal of the *World* of those days for bright, lively writing and for keen local reporting. But the business side was not well-managed, and by 1930 the paper was losing money. In his will, Pulitzer had done his best to forbid sale of the newspaper under any circumstances, but Pulitzer's son, Herbert, had none of his father's dedicated and sentimental love for the *World*. In 1930, Herbert decided to sell the paper.

One of the first men he approached was Adolph Ochs, and he offered to sell him the *World* for $10,000,000.

Ochs was a sick man but his mind was crystal clear. The proposal horrified him, for he felt strongly that ownership of a newspaper entailed an almost sacred responsibility. He pleaded with Herbert to reconsider, suggesting possible ways of revamping the paper to make it more profitable.

"You might try to put out a newspaper like the *Daily Mail* of London," he said, "a newspaper of few pages with news greatly condensed but not sensational. You could keep all the most attractive *World* features; make it a 'snappy' newspaper. I am confident such a publication would be popular. I make this suggestion though I think it may take some circulation from the *Times*."

Herbert Pulitzer was not interested. For the time being, he wanted to sell the morning and Sunday editions and perhaps continue the evening *World* himself.

But Ochs could not in conscience consider spending $10,000,000 for the good name and good will of two editions of the *World,* or even three. "I doubt whether the *Times* would gain a great deal in circulation from consolidation with the *World*," he told Pulitzer. "*World* readers have always had an opportunity to switch to the *Times,* but it wasn't the newspaper that appealed to them. The *World* has educated its readers for many years," he added wryly, "to believe that the *Times* is ultra-conservative, under the influence of big interests and an apologist for Wall Street."

Herbert Pulitzer thought Ochs was merely angling for a lower price. He could not understand that the old man sincerely dreaded the death of a fine newspaper, even a competing newspaper. More spirited than he had been in months,

Ochs tried one more tack. He offered to put up a substantial amount of cash from his own pocket, to help a group of *World* editors to buy the newspaper and run it on their own. He wanted no hand in running the paper, but he was willing to buy some stock in what might become increasingly stiff competition for the *Times*; he could not allow his old enemy's daily to die without trying every cure he could think of.

On this proposal, Pulitzer would not give an immediate answer. Weary from the strain of the conference, Ochs agreed with Effie to leave the next morning for Lake George, but he told his son-in-law to keep after Pulitzer and try to work out some sort of syndicate plan. Sulzberger did his best, but Pulitzer refused to talk about selling the *World* to its editors till he had tried every other potential purchaser. In the winter of 1931, Ochs was on a cruise on the Pacific when Sulzberger cabled him in Hawaii that the Scripps-Howard newspaper chain was about to buy the *World*. Ochs cut his trip short and came right home—too late. The morning and Sunday *World* were already sold, and the evening *World* had been merged with the Scripps-Howard *Telegram*, making a single newspaper, the New York *World-Telegram*.

Ochs felt the grief another man might have felt at losing an old friend. Keyed up beyond his strength, he walked into an editorial conference at the *Times* immediately on arrival in New York, and gave a long, emotional talk about how hard he had tried to save the *World*.

"New York would have supported a newspaper along the lines I suggested," he insisted. "The men on the *World* would have worked their heads off to get out a newspaper in which they had an interest. If I had been here to testify to these things, the court would not have allowed the sale."

With an old man's querulousness, he harped on this theme for months. He brooded over the fact that of almost a score of New York dailies in 1896, only his *Times* now survived on its own, for every other paper had either died or had combined with another. Would the same fate befall the *Times* after he was gone? In these months, he hounded his lawyer to make sure his own will was sufficiently clear about this matter; control of the *Times* must not go out of his immediate family. And he solemnly impressed on his family their duty to continue the newspaper with the same high sense of public service to which it was dedicated during his lifetime.

Then in the autumn of 1931, Ochs had still another weakening blow. On October 26, his brother George died at the age of seventy, three years younger than Adolph himself. George, who had changed his name from Ochs to Oakes during the first World War because the German sound of "Ochs" upset him, had been working with Adolph for many years in New York, editing a current events supplement of the *Times*. Mourning his brother, Adolph knew his own death must be nearing.

But even as he grew frailer physically, Ochs still did not let his mind lapse into the worship of the past to which so many old men succumb when their health fails. Though he was prone to quirky worries now, he looked on the violent upheaval following the stock market crash of 1929 with the eyes of a far-younger man. Though he fretted, without reason, about the financial stability of the *Times*, he still had the mental flexibility to question some of his basic beliefs.

By following his father's advice to "work hard and pay your debts," he himself had risen from poverty and obscurity to riches and eminence. Any other man could have done the same, he had always reasoned. He had never assumed he was wiser than most men or blessed with a quicker mind or a larger store of energy; and he had grown up in a day when many people believed any boy could rise from log cabin to White House if only he tried hard enough. The great depression of the early thirties that put millions on the bread lines through no fault of their own came when Ochs was past seventy and in failing health. But instead of holding on tight to his old ideas, he adopted some new ones.

Perhaps the United States had changed more drastically during his lifetime than he had understood, he decided. In his youth, any boy with push could make his way, but now in the crowded cities could any slum boy have the same chance he himself had had? Could any willing worker still better himself? The hordes of starving unemployed made Ochs doubt his old ideas. Perhaps the government owed its citizens more help in these more complex days. At the age of seventy-four, he abandoned his lifelong conservatism and supported Franklin D. Roosevelt for the Presidency.

This stunning decision to put *The New York Times* in the liberal camp in 1932 was the last major decision made by Adolph Ochs. In 1933, he suffered a serious heart attack, and though he recovered, his doctors forbade any further taxing business activity. Now the melancholy that had oppressed him intermittently in recent years completely stifled his former high spirits. He sat for hours up in White Plains without speaking, and when he spoke it was to mutter gloomy worries. The tragic kidnapping of Charles A. Lindbergh's son set off a nation-wide wave of kidnappings, and Ochs fretted so pitifully about the safety of his own grandchildren that to humor him the young Sulzbergers were sent to England for a time.

Then mysteriously, in the spring of 1935, his spirits rose again. He looked less haggard and shrunken, and he astonished everybody by cheerfully taking an interest in his meals and in visits from old friends. When he was very ill, he had stopped reading the *Times*, but now he started reading it again, even dictating a few gentle memos about stories, and conferring in his library on newspaper matters. Then early in April, he came up with an astonishing notion.

He would go to Chattanooga for a bit, he told Effie. There were a few details about the Chattanooga *Times* he wanted to talk over with his brother and nephews. The dogwoods on the sides of Lookout Mountain would be flowering soon, and he wanted to see them again. Arthur Sulzberger said he would make the trip with him, but with the persistence of a sick old man Ochs insisted on going alone.

He won out at last, but a nurse would have to accompany him. Ochs agreed to this and suggested that since he always loved traveling with young people, he would like his granddaughter Marian to come, too. It was time, now that Marian was sixteen, that he take her on a tour of his happy old haunts down in Tennessee, he said. Unwilling to cross him, Marian's parents agreed to let her accompany him and Marian herself was delighted to go off with Granddaddy, though she couldn't imagine why she was being allowed to miss a few weeks of school this way.

Ochs embarked on the journey with gusto, making sure the party had comfortable connecting compartments on a good train. They had a gay dinner served in their rooms, then played rummy till bedtime. Ochs awoke the next morning refreshed and eagerly ready to show Chattanooga to Marian; and he excitedly pointed out landmarks as they drove from the station to the old house at Cedar and Fifth streets, where his sister, Mrs. Harry Adler, and her family still lived.

Everybody who came to call that Sunday afternoon and evening marveled at how well Adolph looked. Had the reports about his illness been exaggerated? On the long-distance phone that evening, even Effie in New York felt reassured, for his voice sounded so strong and happy.

The next morning, Marian went off for some sightseeing and tennis with her cousins, while Granddaddy and a nephew went down to the office. Ochs insisted on walking through the whole Chattanooga *Times* plant, shaking hands. Then he sat talking over the paper's operation with such keen interest that he had to be reminded when it was time for lunch. With his brother Milton and several editors and his nurse he walked a block to a restaurant, still chatting animatedly.

There was a pause in the conversation after the waiter had passed out menus and they were all deciding what to eat.

"What will you have, Dolph?" Milton asked, without looking up. When there was no answer, Milton repeated his question, then looked up to find Adolph slumped over the table, apparently unconscious.

The nurse quickly administered a hypodermic injection and someone called an ambulance. But Adolph Ochs never recovered consciousness. He died in a hospital several hours later. Marian, who had been summoned from the tennis party with her cousins, wept in the hospital corridor for her whole family.

The death of Adolph Ochs on April 8, 1935, was mourned by more than his family. The following day, all Chattanooga paid him tribute. Every business office closed, every factory shut its doors, even the state legislature in Nashville suspended its session, while a funeral service was held for the great publisher. His brother Milton, his sister Mrs. Adler, and their children joined Marian in representing his family at this service in the city that had been his home for so many years.

Then three days later, in New York, more than 3,000 men and women gathered in Temple Emanu-El on Fifth Avenue for another service honoring Adolph Ochs. Sorrowful relatives who had traveled up from Chattanooga with Ochs on his last trip north joined Effie and the Sulzbergers in the crowded temple. Throughout the nation, the wires of the Associated Press paid silent tribute for two minutes, and other tributes poured in from every quarter. "His great contribution to journalism and to good citizenship will always be remembered," President Franklin D. Roosevelt wrote. "The nation has lost one of its great newspaper geniuses," wired Ochs's old enemy, William Randolph Hearst.

Later, under a cold, gray sky, Ochs was buried at Mount Hope Cemetery in Westchester, not far from the rolling woods of his White Plains home.

A deep sadness filled the building on West Forty-third Street where Adolph Ochs would never again bustle from the elevator with a kindly smile for everyone, a suggestion, a sharp new idea. But *The New York Times* had to appear every morning, and appear it did, solid and respected as a newspaper of unparalleled distinction—a glorious monument to the memory of Adolph S. Ochs.

For some time, Arthur Hays Sulzberger had been in almost complete charge of the paper, ably aided by his cousin-by-marriage, Julius Ochs Adler, and the whole expert team Adolph Ochs had assembled. With the death of Ochs there were no sudden, drastic changes in the newspaper; in fact, plans for brightening the make-up with more pictures were postponed for a year so that no one could say the heirs were changing the character of the *Times*.

This Sulzberger had no intention of doing. *The New York Times* would stay fundamentally as Adolph Ochs had built it—a newspaper aiming at the most complete possible coverage of world events in its news columns and speaking on the editorial page for the fair-minded, liberal-tending conservative point of view.

Arthur Hays Sulzberger had no illusions about his own special qualifications for running *The New York Times*. A man who could laugh at himself, he liked to start a speech before some illustrious group by saying: "Perhaps you wonder how to get to be the publisher of a great newspaper. Let me tell you my own system. Get up early, work hard—and marry the boss's daughter." The laugh this always got was a friendly laugh, though, because Sulzberger's charm immediately disarmed any antagonism. And even more to the point, the decisions he made as the newspaper's chief during the trying days of the New Deal, then through the cataclysm of the second World War, Ochs had shown good judgment in entrusting the *Times* to his son-in-law. With no knowledge at all about newspapering, Sulzberger had learned how to apply the Ochs principles of journalism with complete competence. He did it by hard work and a humble manner. Explaining why he had come into the office six days most weeks, despite the excellent staff he had working for him, he once said: "I didn't want anybody to think I was off playing polo with Mr. Ochs's money."

For twenty-six years he ran the paper, then in 1961, when ill health forced him to slow his own pace, Sulzberger took another lesson from his father-in-law. He appointed his own son-in-law to succeed him as publisher—Orvil E. Dryfoos, Marian's husband, who had spent years working his way through the building from the newsroom to the publisher's office on the fourteenth floor.

Upon Dryfoos's untimely death two years later, in 1963 Ochs's only grandson, Arthur Ochs Sulzberger, moved into the publisher's office at the *Times* when he was just thirty-seven. Called "Punch" by all who know him (the nickname harked back to his childhood closeness to his youngest sister, Judy) he had been expected to spend a good many more years moving from department to department at the newspaper before taking over its direction.

However, "Punch" soon made doubters remember that his grandfather had been almost exactly the same age when he had first taken control of *The New York Times*, and during his three decades at the helm he supervised many major changes that not only preserved the newspaper's stature in the age of computers, but also increased its profits.

In 1992, he decided that it was time to give up his day to day responsibilities, and announced the appointment of his son, Arthur Ochs Sulzberger Jr., as the paper's publisher. Thus it is the great-grandson of Adolph Ochs whose name now appears daily at the head of the list of executives on the editorial page of *The New York Times*.

And in the lobby of the *Times* building on West Forty-third Street, there sits a marble bust of a kindly man somewhat resembling George Washington, inscribed with the words that still guide the newspaper:

"To give the news impartially, without fear or favor, regardless of any party, sect, or interest involved."

Also, up on the fourteenth floor, where the newspaper's top executives have their offices, there still stands a huge grandfather clock with a bronze plaque on it: "To Adolph S. Ochs—From the Citizens of Chattanooga." And it is still ticking.

BIBLIOGRAPHY

Berger, Meyer. *The Story of the New York Times 1851- 1951*. New York: Simon and Schuster, 1951.

Davidson, Donald. "The Tennessee: Frontier to Secession"; "The Tennessee: Civil War to TVA." Rinehart and Company, 1948.

Davis, Elmer. "History of *The New York Times* 1851-1921." *New York Times,* 1921.

Govan, Gilbert E., and Livingood, James W. *The Chattanooga Country*. New York: E. P. Dutton, 1952.

Johnson, Gerald W. *An Honorable Titan*. New York: Harper, 1946.

Mott, Frank L. *American Journalism*. New York: Macmillan, 1941.

Noble, Iris. *Joseph Pulitzer: Front Page Pioneer.* New York: Messner, 1957.

INDEX

Sulzberger in charge, 181-82; Orvil E. Dryfoos succeeds him as publisher, 183; followed by Arthur Ochs Sulzberger, 183; followed by Arthur Ochs Sulzberger, Jr., 183

New York *Tribune*, 19, 74, 89, 90, 105

New York *World*, 81, 89, 96, 101, 106, 107, 127, 137, 174-76

New York *World-Telegram*, 176

"New York's Hundred Neediest Cases," 160-61

Newfoundland, 132, 142

Newspapermaker, the, 93

Noble, Mr., 72

North Pole, 138, 139-41

Northcliffe, Lord, 146

Ochs, Ada (sister), 31; as Mrs. Henry Adler, 87, 180, 181

Ochs, Adolph Simon, his parents, 5, 6, 9-18; sells newspapers, 14, 18, 19; birth of, 15; character and description, 18, 33, 92; clerks in store, 19; works for Knoxville *Chronicle*, 20-26; quits school, 21; plans for his own paper, 23-24, 30; on the *Courier-Journal*, 27-29; on Knoxville *Tribune,* 29; partner in Chattanooga *Dispatch*, 30-32; compiles city directory, 32-34; buys Chattanooga *Times*, 35-36; his statement of policy, 38; borrows money to pay bills, 40-41, 42-45, 48; his family moves to Chattanooga, 45; at 21, 45-46; paper begins to make money, 47; his paper considered outstanding, 48-49; at 24, 50; marriage, 52-53; at White House, 53; death of first two children, 53; his other interests, 54, 56; entertains President Cleveland, 54-55; death of father, 56; buys land, 57-58; in debt again, 58-59; constructs new building for paper, 58-59; borrows money again, 60-63, 68-70; is near bankruptcy, 62; tries to buy another newspaper, 63, 67, 68-70; mortgages new building, 63-64, 66; birth of daughter, 66; opening day at new building, 67-68; looks for a New York newspaper, 70-73; negotiates for *The New York Times,* 75-85; is now its publisher, 85; his competition, 89-90; his statement of aims, 90-92; at 38, 92-93; innovations, 93-94, 113; is praised by trade magazine, 93; thinks up slogan, 96-97; refuses Tammany bribe, 97-98, 102-04; in 1896 presidential campaign, 99-101; his AP membership, 105-06; cuts price of paper, 108-09; gains complete control, 110-11; is debt free, 111; at 42, 112; his first European trip, 114-15; plans new uptown building, 123-25; takes vacations, 126-29; avoids limelight, 129; death of mother, 139; is given gift by staff, 152; marriage of daughter, 153-54; on verge of nervous collapse, 158; is grandfather, 160, 162, 166-67; hires son-in-law, 160-62; celebrates 25th anniversary,

163-165; is not well, 165; works at home, 165; his philanthropy, 168-70; his seventieth birthday, 170; has to slow down, 172-73; tries to save *World*, 175-76; insures family control of *Times*, 177; death of brother George, 177; has heart attack, 178; death, 180; tribute to, 181

Ochs, Bertha Levy (mother), 10-11, 15-18, 29, 43, 50, 56, 72, 86, 95, 126, 138-39

Ochs, George (brother), 17, 31, 54, 87, 114, 177

Ochs Highway, 171

Ochs, Iphigene (wife) 51-54, 61, 63-64, 66, 71-72, 76, 83-85, 86-88, 94, 95, 102, 105, 112, 114-15, 140-41, 158, 159, 165, 170, 172, 176, 179. *See also* Wise, Iphigene Miriam

Ochs, Iphigene (daughter), 6, 66-67, 69, 87-88, 104-05, 115, 121-22, 127, 153-54; marries Arthur Hays Sulzberger, 154. *See also* Sulzberger, Iphigene Ochs

Ochs, Julius (father), 9, 11-14, 15-18, 23, 45, 50, 56

Ochs, Mattie (sister), 31

Ochs, Milton (brother), 31, 54, 87, 180-81

Ochs, Nannie (sister), 31

Ochsenberg, 11

Ohio, 15, 16, 154

Over-the-River Company, 57-58

Pan-American Exposition, 119

Paris, France, 42, 114, 116-17, 146, 157, 165

Park Row, 85, 90, 93, 118

Paul, Franc, 30-31, 32

Peary, Admiral Robert E., 138, 139-41

Philadelphia, Pennsylvania, 137-38

Philadelphia *Public-Ledger*, 137-38

Pittsburgh, Pennsylvania, 49, 55, 57

Poems of Thomas Hood, The, 25

Popham, John N., 7

Port Arthur, 133

Presidential campaign of 1896, 99-102

Princeton University Library, 169

Providence, Rhode Island, 18-19

Pulitzer, Herbert, 174-76

Pulitzer, Joseph, 81, 89-90, 101-02, 105-06, 127, 173-74

Raymond, Henry J., 74, 91, 109, 155

Read, Thomas, 104

Recorder, the, 81, 84, 89

Redfield, D. M., 97

Reed, Dr. Walter, 42

Reick, William, 138

Republicans, 74, 84, 99

Rhode Island, 18, 19

Rome, Italy, 165

Roosevelt, Franklin D., 178, 181

Roosevelt, Theodore, 120, 149

Rostrom, Captain, 145

Rothermere, Viscount, 170

Rule, Captain William, 20-21, 24-26, 162-63, 171

Russia/Russians, 132-35, 150

Russo-Japanese War, 132-36

St. Louis *Post-Dispatch*, 90, 106

San Francisco *Argonaut*, 96

San Francisco, California, 90, 96, 159

Sarajevo, 149

Schiff, Jacob, 83-84

ABOUT THE AUTHOR

Doris Faber came to work on *The New York Times* as a college correspondent in 1942 and became a staff reporter the following year. She retired from the newspaper in 1951 following her marriage to a fellow reporter and devoted her time to raising a family, gardening and writing books. Since then, she has written more than forty books for adults and for young people, mostly about American history or biographies of historical figures, among them *From Printer's Devil to Publisher: Adolph S. Ochs of The New York Times*, published originally in 1963 and updated in 1996. She and her husband have two grown daughters and live on a farm in Columbia County, New York.